D1374132

UNSTUCK

UNSTUCK

A Story About Gaining Perspective, Creating Traction, and Pursuing Your Passion

Dan Webster and Randy Gravitt

WILEY

For general information about our other products and services, please contact our Customer Care Department within the United States at (800) 762-2974, outside the United States at (317) 572-3993 or fax (317) 572-4002.

Wiley publishes in a variety of print and electronic formats and by print-on-demand. Some material included with standard print versions of this book may not be included in e-books or in print-on-demand. If this book refers to media such as a CD or DVD that is not included in the version you purchased, you may download this material at http://booksupport.wiley.com. For more information about Wiley products, visit www.wiley.com.

Library of Congress Cataloging-in-Publication Data is available

Cover Design: Wiley
Cover Image: © FrankRamspott/iStockphoto

Printed in the United States of America

10 9 8 7 6 5 4 3 2 1

I dedicate this project to my co-author,
Randy Gravitt. His life is a living illustration
of this book. He is truly one of the finest
men I've ever met.
—DW

To my wife, Laura.
Your love, prayer, and encouragement
are the reason I am living my dream.
Thank you!
—RG

Contents

Foreword

Have you ever felt stuck in life? I know I have. Years ago, I found myself stalled in my work as well as in my most important relationships. Things appeared hopeless. I almost lost everything that was important to me. Thankfully, I was able to find traction in my life and work, but it took longer than it should have. Looking back, I wish I would have had a copy of UNSTUCK to serve as my compass toward renewal.

As an author and speaker I now have the opportunity to work with organizations and teams all over the world, and I have observed a trend among today's leaders. They, too, have a tendency to lose their way. Not knowing the questions to ask or steps to take in order to move forward often leaves them feeling paralyzed, anxious, and defeated. Can you relate to what I'm saying? If so, I have good news. The book you are holding in your hand is about to help you find renewal. Dan Webster and Randy Gravitt have done a beautiful job capturing the internal conflict felt when someone is stuck while blending guiding principles into the narrative, describing a process of moving forward in the midst of the struggle.

Dan and Randy have spent their lives inspiring others to align their passions, live authentically, and to reach their potential. They are both gifted communicators who understand the process of leader development at the highest level. I have been personally encouraged by their work, and I know you will be too.

So, if you are disengaged in your career, struggling relationally at home, or lacking traction in other areas of your life, I am confident UNSTUCK will become your road map back to the life you are meant to live.

Jon Gordon

Introduction

If you have ever been stuck, you know how frustrating it can be. However, spinning your wheels in a vehicle, buried in the mud, barely compares to a life that has lost traction. A few years ago, both of the authors of this book found ourselves wondering if we were still on the right career paths. The malaise might as well have been mud. Many days felt hopeless as we struggled through the mundane monotony with little hope of renewal at work. Admittedly, there were times that being stuck at work also affected other areas of our lives.

Looking back, we could have settled for the status quo and stayed stuck. Many people make that choice. How about you? Do you feel trapped in a dead-end job, dreading the drudgery of work? Are you merely going through the motions in your relationships with those who matter most? Are you mired in a habit you need to break? If you answered *yes* to any of those, we have good news. You can become UNSTUCK. A fulfilling and significant career is still possible. Your most important relationships can again be life giving and bring you joy. And your life can experience transformation as you leave destructive habits behind and redirect toward growth.

When bogged down, our inclination is to grind it out and try harder. But if you have ever been stuck, you know that pushing the accelerator only buries you deeper in the muck. After discovering that trying harder doesn't work, the temptation can shift to trying less and choosing to disengage. Trying less may feel easier, but it still fails to create progress. The only thing that helps when you are stuck is traction.

Thankfully, we both were eventually able to become UNSTUCK and find renewal in work and life. How did we do it? By applying the principles you are about to read. On the following pages, you will encounter the story of George Johnson, and we think you will be able to relate. Truthfully, there is a bit of George in each of us. We all have a tendency to lose our way.

After you enjoy the story you will be positioned to activate its truths just like we continue to do. We have included an application guide in the back half of the book to walk you through the renewal process. It is a process to help you get UNSTUCK. If you faithfully work the process we are confident it will help you create traction in your life and work too. As you will discover, renewal is available to anyone who chooses to apply the simple formula that helped us.

It's time to for you to get UNSTUCK!

UNSTUCK

The Fable

The STOP Sign

"Anne, we need to talk."

As soon as the words rolled out of George Johnson's mouth, the flashing blue lights caught his attention in the rearview mirror of his Lexus.

You have to be kidding me, came rushing hotly into George's mind. *Of all days and of all …*

The voice of his wife, Anne, interrupted his thinking. "George! You ran the STOP sign!" But it was too late. George had blown right through it, preoccupied with the thoughts that had been building in his mind and heart for weeks. The last thing George expected was to be pulled over in his own neighborhood.

Though once vibrant and fully engaged in his work, the past seven years as the president of First National Bank had taken its toll on George's psyche. He felt like his soul wasn't in his work anymore. Board meetings, golf outings, loan approvals, regulatory issues, meaningless emails, and monitoring his 401(k) statements consumed most of his time. George knew in his gut there was more to life than these things, but he didn't feel fulfilled by the work he was doing. Significance was eluding him.

"May I see your license and registration please?"

Not recognizing the young officer, George's eyes lowered to the name badge over the right shirt pocket of his freshly starched uniform, which read, simply, BRADLEY.

"Sir, I live in this neighborhood. Less than a mile from here, in fact."

Without emotion, the officer replied, "Then you should know children play on these streets and cross at this intersection all the time. The STOP sign applies to everyone, sir. Now if I could see your license and registration please."

"I'm the president of the bank, and we have lived in this subdivision for thirteen years," George pointed out, glancing over at his wife. The fact that Anne sat quietly didn't stop her from communicating her disapproval to her husband. With just one slightly raised eyebrow she relayed that George needed to obey the officer's request.

"Sir, I am not going to ask you again. Your license and registration." This time, there was little patience in Bradley's tone. Reluctantly, George complied.

For the next ten minutes neither George nor Anne said a word. It was all he could do to keep from exploding. *A ticket in my own neighborhood. This is ridiculous!* The fact that three of his neighbors drove by, slowing down to see what had happened, didn't help matters.

"Sign here, please," were the next words George heard. "Your signature is not an admission of guilt. If you choose to dispute the charges, you have the right to appear in court on June 20."

Mumbling under his breath, George scribbled his name.

Confession

The house felt empty as George walked through the door leading from the garage to the kitchen.

Following him into the house, Anne asked, "What is it you want to talk about?," not forgetting his words prior to the STOP sign.

"Not now, Anne."

"I really want to talk about what's on your mind," she said with a touch of concern.

"It's nothing, really."

"George, you said we need to talk; now let's have it."

Realizing this woman who knew him so well was not about to let it go, George showed a crack in the façade of strength he was trying to portray.

"I'm losing it, Anne."

"Losing what, dear?"

"My mind, I think."

"Come on, George. You've pushed the limits on that STOP sign for years. I hate to say it, but the officer had no choice. I'm not upset; let it go and let's get some rest."

"Anne, I'm not talking about the STOP sign. I'm talking about me. Something is wrong with me."

Never one to complain, the way George said that last sentence communicated a sense of fear, almost a cry for help. Frankly, it scared Anne, who turned toward the kitchen as she said, "Sit down and I'll put on a kettle of tea."

As George and Anne talked well into the night, it was obvious something was wrong. George unloaded the emptiness, boredom, and confusion he was feeling about his life. There were times when Anne questioned whether it was simply a phase George was going through, but she mostly just listened. When they eventually went to bed, it was 1:37 in the morning and George was more than tired. He was weary.

George showed a crack in the façade of strength he was trying to portray.

Sunday morning dawned with George still exhausted, emotionally spent from his late night confession. At breakfast, Anne poured George's coffee with the gentle suggestion, "You need to talk with someone, sweetheart. Someone who can help you process what you are feeling. I have to believe this is simply a phase. You have always loved your work, and frankly your life."

"Who would I talk to? Are you suggesting a shrink?"

"Maybe. I don't know. Someone who can be objective. A counselor or maybe even the reverend. You need help, George; all of this despair is not like you."

As Anne walked back over to the coffeemaker to return the pot, George felt a surge of anger coupled with despair. He knew she was right. He needed help.

Back at the Bank

Patty Porter was usually the second to show up each morning at First National Bank. That had been true pretty much every morning until recently. Wondering, again, where George was, she flipped on the lights and fired up the computer system to prepare for the tellers who were soon to arrive. *George is coming in later and later each day*, she thought as she opened the office door of her longtime boss. Everyone at First National knew Patty was the glue that held the place together. At least it had felt that way for the past couple of years.

Something in George had changed, and everyone sensed it. Patty, however, was as steady as ever. She approached each day with energy and enthusiasm, always the first to offer a word of encouragement or to pitch in when things backed up.

Maureen had recently felt the impact of Patty's presence. She was the newest teller and worked only on Tuesday and Thursday afternoons. When her mom was diagnosed with cancer, Patty was the first from the bank to pay a visit. Patty had even served Maureen's mom recently by driving her to a chemo treatment on a day when Maureen had a stomach bug.

Patty was just that way. The bank was more than a job to her. It was a place to live out her passion for people. She planned the celebrations, baked the cookies, visited employees when they were sick, and even attended the ball games and recitals of her coworkers' children. Yes, Patty was the glue.

George arrived just after the second teller showed up. "I was about to call 911, George. You okay?"

"I'm fine. Just a long weekend with graduation and everything."

"I bet. How is Anne? She must be so proud of Mark. He looked great walking across that stage."

"She's fine. We appreciate you guys for making the time to drive over," George replied tersely.

"Are you kidding? There is no way we would have missed it."

As Patty turned and walked back to her outer office she knew George was struggling and that those around him were feeling the effects. For the first time, she was truly worried about her boss.

Losing Heart

Midway through the morning an email arrived that sent George over the edge. It was a bill from Morton Frazier. The company George contracted to do repairs on the building had just completed its annual touch-ups on the exterior of the bank. The invoice included an additional $200 charge for a gutter repair that had not been authorized. The gutters had been damaged by a spring storm and needed an overhaul, but it was the principle of the thing for George. "How can Morton charge me two hundred dollars for those gutters when he didn't even ask me to approve the repair?"

Hearing George talking to himself in a loud tone, Patty stepped to his office door. "You did need them repaired, didn't you?"

"Well, yeah. But I didn't tell Morton to do it."

"George, what's wrong with you? Morton always does our repairs and at a very reasonable rate, and the gutters look great."

"Yeah, well he should have asked first."

"It would crush him if he thought you felt he was taking advantage of us. He is still so grateful for the loan you helped his family get on their first house. He told me the other day you're still his favorite customer. Maybe he has a lot on his mind and he just forgot to ask?"

"What would he have on his mind?"

"His wife is dealing with a lot right now. Their youngest son, Tyler, is disabled, and she is trying to help him transition into school. I'm sure that is affecting Morton too.

"How do you know all that?"

"I visited with them last Thursday night when I dropped off their dinner," Patty replied. "Paula said it has been a very challenging time for their family."

"Paula?" George interrupted.

"Morton's wife. She's so strong and such a great mom," Patty stated as if she were a member of the Frazier family.

"Well, that's beside the point. He should have sought approval of the work before it was done. He clearly doesn't value this relationship. Perhaps it's time we find a new contractor."

"My, oh my. I never thought I would live to see the day that the most generous and understanding man I know would react this way to something so inconsequential." Patty challenged as she sat down in the chair in front of George's desk. "How is it you are ready to sever ties to a great friend and contractor so swiftly over something so insignificant?"

Patty's words stung George, especially coming from her. There was no one at the bank George respected more than Patty. During their time together at First National, Patty had rarely challenged him the way she just had. There was a tone of disappointment in her words. George had never known Patty to be negative with anyone. He thought, *I must really be in a bad place if Patty is so upset.* He found himself wanting to run out of the bank forever, knowing he was only going through the motions in his work. He felt like a fraud. He felt guilty about accusing

Morton Frazier of being anything but honest. He had known Morton for years. A wave of shame came over him.

George thought back to the first time he met Morton. He recalled the rickety old truck easing into the bank. He had been returning from grabbing lunch as Morton pulled in with a flat tire. George even remembered their conversation.

"Looks like you're having a little trouble there... Anything I can help you with?"

"Nah. Just a flat tire. If you don't mind me taking a parking space, I'll change it and be out of your way in no time."

"Of course. Nice truck, by the way." George said, admiring the lines of the classic Chevy.

"Yeah, she's on her last legs, but I've got to keep her running to haul around my stuff."

George had noticed paint buckets and a ladder attached to a rusty old bracket on the bed of the truck.

"Guess it would be pretty hard to part with a truck like this?"

"Not as hard as you think. Make me an offer. I've been trying to upgrade for the last eight months but haven't been able to make it happen."

Morton had proceeded to share with George his vision of having multiple crews and a two-truck operation, one for painting jobs and one for general home improvement and remodeling.

George was impressed. After discussing some of the financials of the business, not only had George offered to work with Morton to secure a loan to expand the business, he also had bought Morton's truck.

"I've been needing a pickup to haul firewood, and this baby will be perfect for teaching my boys to drive."

"How old are your boys?" Morton asked.

"Ten and eight, but I'll put it to good use between now and when they get their permits."

After the deals were made, George hired Morton to do maintenance work around the bank. The two-truck operation quickly became a reality and Morton's business went on to thrive. The old Chevy proved to be a good purchase because both his boys had learned to handle its manual transmission before they graduated from high school.

As he reminisced about his meeting with Morton all those years ago, George felt a wave of remorse wash over him. "What can I say, Patty?" George asked, hoping to end the exchange. "You're right. I'll give Morton a call."

"Excuse me if I'm out of line, but I don't think this has anything to do with the bill or Morton. This is about you, George. You have changed. Morton wasn't the only one you helped."

"What do you mean?"

"Remember the Parkers? They had no business being given a chance to open their bed and breakfast, yet you are the one who told me, 'There's something about them. I think they have what it takes to make a go of it.' Remember how they got their loan? I recall you sending them over to American Bank, so you could cosign for them. . . . You, George."

She continued, "And when Tim Jensen expanded his plumbing shop and bought his warehouse, I remember a certain banker and his two little boys showing up on a Saturday morning and helping Tim clean the place."

Patty reeled off a couple of other individuals George had helped and said, "That is who you are, George. Those people were given a start because of you. You might want to open the door of your cabinet and take a look at your heart again."

Tucked in the back of George's credenza in his office was an award in the shape of a heart. It had been given to him by the city council a couple of years after the bank opened. Patty walked across the office, opened the door and reached behind a stack of binders and found it. She gently brushed a layer of dust from the top of the crystal figure before placing it on the desk in front of George.

George had always felt awkward keeping it on display. He fixed his gaze on the words etched into the front of the figure:

Presented to George Johnson
"The HEART of the Community"

"It was awesome, George. When you received that award, I knew I made the right decision when I came over with you from Conroy. How many times did I hear you say in those first few years, 'We are going to be the bank with a heart'? That little piece of Waterford validated that you—that we—were on the right track."

"I went home and told Paul that you reminded me of George Bailey from *It's a Wonderful Life*—always looking out for the underdog, using your amazing financial mind to help others have a better life and future."

Finishing the sentence, Patty pointed at the heart-shaped crystal in front of George. "You need to find your heart again, George." Her words had an encouraging tone. As she turned and headed out the door, the phone on George's desk began to ring.

The Phone Call

"Good morning, George, Jim Clarke, here. How's it going my new friend?" came the voice through the receiver.

George was caught off guard by the voice on the other end of the call. Jim Clarke was the last person George was expecting to hear from that morning. Jim was the owner of The Wake Up coffee shop in the town where George's son Mark had attended school. In fact, Jim had been instrumental in helping Mark navigate his last semester of college and land an important internship on a path toward a career in architecture. Jim's influence had even been a catalyst for an improved relationship between George and Mark. Things had been shaky when Mark considered changing his major in the middle of his senior year. Jim took Mark through a process of discovery he had labeled "Finding Your Way." Mark clearly had benefited from Jim and truly appeared to be on the right path.

"What's up, Jim? Everything okay?" George asked with a touch of concern. He wondered whether anything was going on with Mark, who was still living in Jim's town and working for Jim's former employer Regents Credit Union. Years ago Jim had cofounded Regents with a man named Daniel Williams. Regents was now adding a new facility, and just last week Daniel had hired Mark as an intern to help him manage a construction project by working with the architect and the contractor. Mark was also starting a graduate degree with a concentration in architecture and design.

"Everything's great, George. Mark came by The Wake Up this morning on his way to Regents. The boy was about to burst with excitement. Today is his first day on the job. He had a set of rolled-up blueprints in his hand, and you would have thought they were gold the way he handled them. It reminded me of the day they delivered my first espresso machine to The Wake. I don't think I slept the night before or the couple of nights after for that matter. Sampling all that espresso had its effects! Passion is a beautiful thing, huh George?" Jim finished with joy in his voice.

George's left eye began to water first. The right was not far behind. As the first tear rolled down his cheek, he felt ambushed by a wave of emotion. The mixture of his personal misery, the idea of Mark being happy, and the feeling of indebtedness he felt toward Jim was almost more than George could handle. He wiped his eyes, pushing the emotion back beneath the surface before he responded.

"I know. Mark texted Anne yesterday afternoon and said he feels like he won the lottery with this opportunity. I really appreciate all you did these past few months to encourage him. I don't know where we would be without your investment in him."

"It was my pleasure. Mark is an amazing young man. You and Anne did a fine job raising him. I have a feeling he is going to flourish in whatever he does."

"I sure hope so."

"I know. Sarah and I were discussing the same thing about Katie just last night."

He wiped his eyes, pushing the emotion back
beneath the surface.

Jim's daughter Katie had graduated with Mark two days earlier. She had been a genuine friend to Mark when he was struggling to navigate his future during their last semester at the university. Jim and his wife Sarah had done a fantastic job encouraging Katie to follow her passion toward finance.

George, however, had not been such a gracious father. He had pushed Mark toward finance, and it had nearly broken their relationship.

"Listen, George, the reason I'm calling is twofold. First, Sarah and I had a good time with you guys at graduation on Saturday. It was great finally meeting you, and I wanted to let you know I appreciate your support of Mark as he seeks to find his way. He told me you have been very encouraging toward him since spring break."

George reflected back on his relationship with Mark over the past several months. He wondered how much Mark had revealed to Jim. It had indeed been rocky between Christmas and the middle of the semester. Christmas was when Mark had revealed he thought he was in the wrong major. After four years of hefty tuition payments, George had flipped out at Mark's revelation.

Finally after spring break, thanks partly to Jim, things between George and Mark improved dramatically.

Jim continued, "The reason I'm calling is to let you know I'm going to be in your area in a couple of weeks, and I was wondering if I could buy you breakfast and pick your brain about something. I thought it would be great to get to know you better, but I'm also hoping you might be able to give me some advice."

"Advice from me? About what?" George asked, a bit intrigued.

"I have been thinking about expanding my business. As you know I run a coffee shop near the university. I always hoped we would eventually be operating multiple locations, but initially Sarah and I agreed that we would only open one location until I proved I could make a go of it. Now, we are at a point in the business where we are ready to scale and add a second location. I have two options for expansion, and both seem to make sense. Frankly, I don't trust myself to make this decision alone. I need a couple of people who understand business and who are not emotionally invested or biased. I have a meeting set up with my former business partner, Daniel Williams, whom you met on Saturday. With our history, there is no one I trust more than Daniel. But honestly, I need someone who can provide an impartial evaluation of the opportunities. You have been around business for a long time, and you have experience with risk and finance." Jim paused with slight admiration in his voice. "So what do you say? You open for a meeting?"

"I don't know what to say," George responded with a hint of excitement. "I'm flattered. I'd be happy to meet and discuss your plans. Name the time and place, and I'll be there."

"Great. How about we connect in two weeks? One of my suppliers is down in your area. I'm scheduled to meet with them on the seventeenth of June. I'll be in late on Sunday night. Could you be free for a breakfast meeting at eight o'clock on Monday? You name the place, and I'll treat."

"The seventeenth works perfectly," George replied without even checking his schedule. Anything he had could be cleared. The reality was there would not be anything of importance on his schedule. It would be another meaningless Monday in a string of meaningless Mondays. "It will give me something to look forward to," George blurted out, exposing a hint of desperation.

Jim picked up on it and left the words hanging before he responded. "You okay, George?"

"Yeah, I'm fine, just an emotional morning," George answered out of character.

Jim discerned something more was affecting George. "Anything I can help with?"

Coming from anyone else, the question would have felt awkward. However, even though Jim was almost a stranger, the way he asked, coupled with the context of the conversation they were having and the fact that George was staring at the crystal heart on his desk, made him feel safe.

George surprised himself with his answer. "I feel like I've lost sight of my purpose."

The next couple of minutes George opened up to Jim about some of the malaise he was feeling toward his work and life in general. Jim listened and encouraged George appropriately. By the end of the call it was clear the meeting on the seventeenth would be good for both of them.

"Listen, George. I don't want to over simplify things here, but I might be able to shed some light on your situation. A few years back I was dealing with something similar to what you are feeling. When we meet, I'd be happy to share with you the things that helped me get back on track. My story might aid you with your current perspective."

The next couple of minutes George opened up to Jim about some of the malaise he was feeling toward his work and life in general.

Even though there was no judgment in Jim's tone, George felt self-conscious about telling Jim what he was feeling. Sure, he liked the idea of discussing his issues with Jim rather than going to therapy, but it all felt unsettling. He dismissed the thought and told Jim he looked forward to the meeting.

Jim encouraged him to hang in there and then expressed his appreciation for George's willingness to serve as a business sounding board. "Thanks, George. I really look forward to connecting in a couple of weeks. Text me the address once you choose a place."

As quickly as the tears had come moments earlier, George felt another wave of emotion as they ended the call. It was partly dread with the thought of opening up to Jim, but mainly he felt a ray of hope surrounding the chance to help someone with a new business idea. That had always been something George was passionate about. Jim's request caused the first flutter in George's heart in what seemed like years. It would not be the last.

Warning Sign

On Thursday afternoon, George went to the gym for a game of racquetball with his neighbor Tom Murray. Tom was also George's attorney and had been a friend for years. Not having exercised in weeks when Tom called with the invitation, George thought it would be a good opportunity to burn a few calories. Within ten minutes, George began to feel light-headed. His heart felt like it would explode. After Tom dove for a shot and hit a beautiful winner, he turned to find George leaning against the back wall trying to catch his breath.

"You okay, George? You don't look so good."

"I don't feel so good. I think I'm done for today."

"Do you want me to call for help?"

"No, I think I'm all right. Just a bit dizzy. Give me a second."

After a couple of minutes George regained his balance, but it was obvious something was wrong.

"You need to go get checked out, George. No need to take a chance. Why don't you let me drive you to Sam's office and have him check you out?" Tom suggested, referring to their friend and physician Dr. Samuel Anderson.

George hated the thought of going to the doctor, but he hated the idea of dying even more.

"I guess so, but I really think I'm okay. I don't want to alarm Anne until after we see Sam."

Tom agreed, and they headed across town to the clinic.

Dr. Anderson conducted a stress test and concluded George's ticker was perfectly fine. His hunch was that it was stress related—perhaps the emotional effects of fatigue, coupled with not enough sleep or exercise, leading the biggest bank in town, and experiencing a family transition.

"I see it all the time. This is a warning, George—a sort of STOP sign, if you will. You need to take care of yourself, or the next time it could be worse."

He tried to process it all, but couldn't find the energy to think about it anymore. The thought of going home and "discussing" the day with Anne made him even more weary. What he really wanted was to escape. A week in the mountains ... perhaps even a few days on a lake with a fishing rod in his hand. George had not fished in years, but he was feeling desperate.

He was awakened from his fantasy with Dr. Anderson's voice. "Please tell Patty thanks for me."

"Patty? What did she do for you?"

"Not for me, actually. It's for my mom. Patty stops by and checks on her a couple of afternoons each week on her way home. She lives two streets over from Mom."

Tom asked, "How is your mom doing, Sam?"

"She's hanging in there. Still lives alone, but she is showing beginning signs of dementia. She's been in that house for nearly forty years. We are trying to talk her in to moving in with us, but she's holding out for now."

"She's a real trooper," Tom acknowledged.

"Seriously, George. Thank Patty. It really helps out for Mom to have company. Patty even drove her over to the cemetery a few weeks ago to visit Dad's grave. Mom likes to go and check on him occasionally even though it has been nearly twenty years since he died. They were married forty-eight years."

"That's a long time to put up with your dad," Tom said in a friendly tone.

"That's a fact," Sam agreed. "Dad was a piece of work."

The men shook hands as Sam reminded George, "Slow down, my friend."

George found himself going through the motions in every area of his life. To say he was disengaged would be an understatement.

Tom and George left the doctor's office ninety minutes later, relieved that George did not have anything wrong with his heart. Tom dropped George off at his car, which they had left in the gym parking lot. As he drove home, George wondered what was wrong with him. He had a sense that everything that was happening was somehow related. When he arrived at home, Anne had dinner waiting. He avoided telling her what had happened at the gym and the subsequent trip to the doctor until after dinner. He was tempted to avoid it altogether, but finally opened up to his wife. To his surprise, Anne was understanding, although her concern was growing.

Over the next few days he found himself going through the motions in every area of his life. To say he was disengaged would be an understatement. Other than anticipating the upcoming meeting with Jim Clarke, he felt unneeded and unmotivated.

Alive, but Not Living

George arrived at the coffee shop ten minutes before his 8:00 AM meeting with Jim Clarke. As he walked in, he noticed Jim sitting quietly at a table by the window writing in a notebook. George grabbed a dark roast coffee and joined him.

"Great to see you, Jim. Thanks again for the invite. I've been looking forward to this."

"Not a problem, George. Good to see you too. Are you guys having a good summer?

"Not too bad so far. We could use a bit of rain," George countered with surface conversation.

"Any plans for the Fourth of July weekend?"

Without much enthusiasm, George responded, "We are putting together a cookout. We'll light the barbecue, have some people over ..." George's voice dropped off as he finished his sentence.

Then slightly raising his voice he asked, "What about you, Jim? Have any big plans?"

"For years our neighborhood has blocked off the street and we do a big cookout. The younger kids decorate their bikes and they put on a little parade for the adults. It's a bunch of fun. Then, when it gets dark, we all walk to a park to watch a fireworks display put on by the city. It's been a great tradition."

George smiled. "Sounds like a good thing."

Jim responded, "It is. The kids love it. Hey, I've been thinking about you since our call a couple of weeks ago,

41

and I do want to discuss my business expansion idea, but if I can ask, what do you think is going on with you right now?"

Though Jim's question felt abrupt, George responded honestly. "Good question, and thanks for your interest. I wish I knew. I've just found myself feeling a bit out of it lately. I guess I'm wondering whose life I'm living right now. I know it is such a strange thought, but I find myself wondering, am I really living *my* life? I mean, why did I choose the vocation I'm in? Why did I go into finance and banking in the first place? Was that really *my* passion or just a move to be financially secure? Even the parts of my work that were the most fulfilling and enjoyable now feel like drudgery and I have no idea why. I feel silly even talking about this stuff, Jim, but I can't shake the haunting feeling that something is wrong inside me. This must sound crazy. This is the kind of stuff that happens to others, not me. By all accounts, I have a wonderful life. I've been successful in my career. I have a great marriage and family. Truthfully, I'm embarrassed to feel this way when there are others with so much less who are grateful and content for what they have. I can't think of a good reason for why I should be like this. Any thoughts on why I am?"

"I don't think anyone is immune from feeling this way. No matter how much you've accomplished or how hard you've worked for the life you've built for yourself ..."

Only partially listening to Jim's response, George interrupted. "It's a heck of a thing, Jim. Everything on the surface of my life glitters right now. I'm healthy. The bank I helped start is humming along. My name is on the front door, for goodness sake. I have a high-performance staff who loves what they do so there's rarely any work-place drama to deal with. I make enough money, maybe even more than I should. Anne and I recently celebrated another wedding anniversary, and we are doing really well. Both our sons are on the right track as they move into their futures. And, add to all this, I purchased the car of my dreams recently. It's a new Lexus, and it's flat out the nicest vehicle I've ever owned. Anyone with so much going so well would be grateful. I should have nothing to complain about." George explained.

"But …," Jim invited.

"But, all the external good things in my life seem to be overshadowed by an inner discontent. It's frustrating—confusing—shameful—I'm embarrassed and I'm mad at myself that I can't get over it. And, to be honest, the way I feel scares me. I am finding myself regretting decisions that I have made and I worry it's too late to make any changes or find happiness again. I would understand these feelings more if the bank was in trouble *or* Anne was leav-ing me *or* one of my sons was ill or worse."

George kept going, "It's becoming difficult for my wife as well. Anne can see it in me, and she has told me more than once I need to go find my smile again. Even Patty, my administrative assistant at the bank, has been commenting recently on how distracted I seem. She has worked with me for fifteen years going all the way back to my time at Conroy Investment. You mentioned in our phone call you might be able to shed some light on my situation. If you can, I'd be grateful."

Jim paused before responding. He wanted to give George more time to talk if that's what he needed. As he listened to his new friend, he could sense that George felt his life had curled up into one huge question mark and that he had no idea how to answer it.

George was sensing the discomfort and embarrassment of feeling vulnerable and out of control.

As the two men sat quietly for a moment, each was thinking completely different thoughts.

Jim was reflecting on how his own life experience could help George. It wasn't that long ago that Jim had found himself in a similar situation at the Regents Credit Union, a company he had cofounded. He and his buddy, Daniel Williams, had built the new business from the ground up. In Regents, Jim thought he had found the job of his dreams, only to discover one year later that he was miserable. His misery was caused by a misalignment with who he was and the role he was required to fill within his company. On the front end of that business there was simply too much systems work and not enough people work. That ended up both weakening Jim's spirit and draining his joy. Selling his portion of the business to Daniel, and entering his own renewal process, saved his life and future. Years later, he was able to recognize the suffering of those difficult days—the *inner discontent* as George had defined it—had been a great teacher. The pain Jim experienced during that time had forced him to face truths about both himself and his goals that would shape his future. *Did George possess the humility and courage to enter a similar process?* Jim wondered.

On the other side of the table, George was sensing the discomfort and embarrassment of feeling vulnerable and out of control. He had pretty much always sat on the control side of the table. He liked feeling weak about as much as having a root canal at the dentist. Opening up to Jim about his life felt awkward and uncomfortable to him. He was pondering how foolish this decision might have been. His thoughts strayed to … *I must look like a complete idiot. Why am I telling this guy all my woes? I should just shut up, pretend I'm okay, and get out of here.*

As George drifted deeper into his thoughts, Jim decided to share his story.

"I feel for you, George. You aren't the first person to go through a time like this. I've owned and operated the Wake Up coffee shop a couple blocks from the University in my town for over fifteen years. During that time I've befriended hundreds of people that include students, professionals in the market place, and professors from the University. I can't count the number of hours I've sat and listened to the life stories of these wonderful people. As I've gotten to know them, no matter their age, many have confided in me seasons of difficulty or frustration. In many ways my own story is similar to many of theirs, and also to yours."

"How is that?" George questioned.

"It wasn't that long ago that I went through a similar—let me call it—*soul storm.* I remember how difficult it was to put my truth on the table and look at it. The truth was my contentment—joy—fulfillment—motivation—whatever you want to call it, had vanished and been replaced by uneasiness. I was miserable. That misery eventually led me to leave Regents Credit Union and to open a different business. The experience of opening a coffee shop ignited a lot of thought, research, and reflecting. I'd love to share with you what I learned if you are up for it. It will take a few minutes to give you the overview. What do you think?"

George paused, looked out the shop window, and concluded, *What do I have to lose? I've already admitted I'm a mess. Maybe Jim is the best option I have right now to find my way to renewal.* And with that, he looked at Jim and admitted, "I'd be grateful to hear more, but let's make sure we leave time to discuss your business questions."

Jim agreed. He leaned down to pull a notebook out of his satchel and tore out a blank sheet of paper. He began to sketch a diagram that would change how George saw his future.

Perspective

George watched Jim attempt to sketch something that looked like a pie chart.

"You aren't related to Leonardo da Vinci, are you, Jim?" George quipped as he watched him struggle to draw two stick figures.

"Nope, but my cousin sent me a postcard from Italy on her honeymoon, so I think that qualifies me to create this little artistic beauty," Jim responded with a grin.

Kiddingly, George said, "Take your time, friend. This place doesn't close for another ten hours."

As Jim put the finishing touches on his masterpiece, he said, "That should just about do it. You ready to be wowed?"

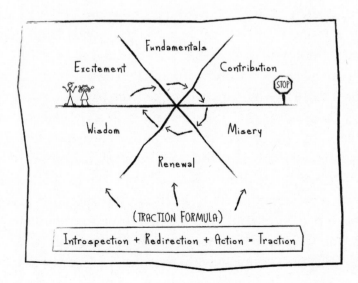

Turning the sketch so George could see it, Jim shifted to a more instructive tone and began the explanation of his drawing.

"George, before we discuss what I call the traction formula, I think it would be helpful to take a step back and consider how life tends to unfold for most people. This little pie-shaped construct helps me remember six phases of life development I have experienced. My understanding of these phases grew out of nearly two decades of personal experience, talking to people at the Wake Up, reading extensively about life process, discussing my life in a counselor's office for a season, and picking the brains of some really smart professors at the university. As we talk through this I think you will see how relevant the traction formula is to every phase. It's been helpful to me, and I hope, it will help you," Jim shared.

"Sounds good," George replied.

Jim continued, pointing to the drawing, "That couple on the left end of the horizontal line represents you and Anne at age twenty-five when you graduated from business school with your MBA. You're the one in the baseball cap in case you wondered. Anne is the one in the dress. That's close to what you two looked like back then, right?"

"It's not far off," George said with a chuckle. "Anne looks about the same. I'm a few pounds heavier, but I still have that baseball cap. Today, it hides my bald spot."

"I hear that," Jim responded as he ran his hand over his own receding hairline. "Each of these pie slices represents a period of time in our life. Do you remember the day you were hired at your first job?" Jim asked.

"Sure," George quickly answered. "Conroy Investment Firm. They hired two people that year. More than fifty people applied for those two jobs. A woman who had graduated from Harvard and I were the two candidates who landed the positions. I'm still not exactly sure why they chose me. Bottom line, I was grateful they did."

"I can imagine. I bet you were fired up to get a job that was both in your interest area and one for which your degree prepared you."

"Absolutely. Both Anne and I were thrilled."

"Most people starting out in their careers experience an *excitement phase*. You get hired, draw a paycheck, and are off and running in your vocation. Being in your twenties, you have a ton of energy to focus on your career, and you have the drive to excel. This is a wonderful time for most of us."

"Those were great days, no doubt. It was exciting, and I was the first one in the office most mornings," George remembered.

"How long did it take in your job at Conroy before you encountered a person, problem, or situation that exposed the fact that you still had a lot to learn?"

"About ten minutes," George answered with a laugh. "In the first week, I discovered my MBA education gave me a handle on a few of the basics, but there were all sorts of things I still needed to get my head around and learn."

"Exactly," Jim agreed. "In every job there is a set of fundamentals a person must grasp if they are to move ahead in their vocation. How quickly those get identified, learned, and mastered has a lot to say about how fast a person becomes successful. In this phase you prepare to make your contribution by increasing your capability. Most of us put our head down and do everything we can to learn and grow—this is the *fundamentals phase*. How long did it take before it felt like you had your head around your job well enough to make a significant contribution to your clients and the firm?"

"It can be challenging to stay passionate about your vocation . . . The routine of work can beat a person down over time."

George responded, "It took a number of years before I truly learned the ropes and felt like I was on top of things. By then I had built a client base and the knowledge that enabled me to begin making money for my clients, myself, and the firm. It takes longer for some to pick things up; a few do it more quickly," George admitted.

"So, after a few years of preparation, you entered the *contribution phase* where you were able to do what you had been trained and prepared to do. By this time you had matured and developed competence. You successfully utilized your experience and brought what you learned to your career on a daily basis. Developing yourself was critical for impact and contribution. By this time, core lessons had been ingested, competence had been achieved, and your talent was impacting the business in a productive way. It can be challenging to stay passionate about your vocation in this phase, because it's not new and exciting any longer," Jim explained. "Does that sound familiar so far?"

George responded, "It does. The routine of work can beat a person down over time. It seems like most people would have been working for a while by the time they hit this phase. What phase comes next? I see a STOP sign there on the right end of the line. What does that mean?"

As George asked the question, both men were startled by the loud screaming sound of multiple sirens outside the coffee shop. They paused and turned to see a fire truck, two police cars, and an ambulance speed right through the STOP sign at the intersection outside the front window.

"Must be a bad accident," George commented.

Jim nodded in agreement.

"Did you see those first responders blow right through that STOP sign?" Jim asked.

"Sure did. Could they make those sirens any louder?"

Jim turned back and asked, "Hey George, here's a question for you. What's the purpose of a STOP sign?"

"Is this a trick question?"

"No, seriously. What is a STOP sign for?"

"I'm gonna go out on a limb and say it's there to get people's attention that they need to *stop*," George stated with a curious expression on his face.

"Have you ever run a STOP sign?"

"Oh man, don't get me started. I recently got pulled over for running a STOP sign. I was, shall we say, a bit preoccupied, lost in my thoughts, and I blew right through one," George admitted.

"Did you get pulled over?"

"Yep. In my own neighborhood. Of course, all of our neighbors seemed to be heading home at that time as well and saw us being pulled over. It was quite embarrassing."

"Ouch. Did you get a ticket?"

"Yeah. It was an expensive mistake."

"Sounds like," Jim agreed. "In this part of the drawing I state what may, or may not, seem obvious. The purpose of a STOP sign is to get our attention. When an inner shift occurs, and feelings of unhappiness or discontent sneak in, those feelings are trying to wake us up to something. Does that sound familiar, George?"

"Are you telling me my feelings of being discontent and my current misery are like a big red STOP sign saying, *Slow down?*" George asked.

"Bingo! But many people choose to ignore STOP signs to their own detriment. Even when a voice from within cries out and says, *Hey pal, pay attention to me. Something isn't right and you need to listen.*"

Jim continued, "There are many different ways to deal with an unexpected and unwanted STOP sign. You can ignore it, deny that it's there, or just pretend nothing is wrong. Some try to irrigate the discomfort by pleasuring the pain away. Some manage it by running back to the excitement phase and taking a new job or engaging a new project. None of those options move a person toward renewal."

"Honestly, George, the best option for those who long for renewal is to walk through the *misery phase*. Sounds fun, huh?" Jim quipped with a sarcastic smile.

"I think I might already know a little about that phase. As a matter of fact, I'm guessing that's the phase I'm currently in," George acknowledged.

"I think you're right. Let me throw something out here. When you started your career I'll bet you thought to yourself, *If I could ever become part owner of a successful bank, be in charge of the place, make a bunch of money, and help people along the way, I'd be happy,*" Jim offered.

"You're right, Jim. I've had that thought more often than I want to admit."

"If I'm right, all those things have come true—yes? You are part owner and president of a successful bank. You are well compensated. And you have helped lots of people along the way."

"Yes, all that is true."

"Then why aren't you the happiest guy in the world, George?"

The question pressed into George's chest. He grimaced before answering. "I'm not sure. Isn't that why we are talking?"

Jim allowed the question to hang in the air before responding.

"Listen, George. What you are feeling is what one feels in the misery phase. Think about it. Everything in your life is as you hoped it would become, and now that you have arrived, you have discovered you aren't happy. That's misery! Some get to misery because things are terrible in their life. That's not true with you.

"Everything in your life is as you hoped it would become, and now that you have arrived, you have discovered you aren't happy. That's misery!"

"Misery manifests itself in many ways. Some experience an overwhelming sense of boredom. They have done the same work for years and the routine has drained their enthusiasm for life. Others feel fatigue on a soul level. They have allowed their work to take more than it should from them, leaving them exhausted. Still others confess they are completely disillusioned. They got the job they longed for and thought it would bring lasting joy, but it hasn't. Along the way either they changed, or the job changed. Here's the deal, George. Misery can shut us down or open us up to consider some really important questions. The purpose of the misery phase is to face what is making us unhappy, to reflect honestly on what's going on, and to identify sacred questions that need to be answered before we can move ahead," Jim emphasized. "I think this is the phase you are in and this is what you need to do."

"Sacred questions? What type of questions are those?" George asked as he leaned back.

"A sacred question is one, that if answered, can help you understand how to find your way to renewal. I'll tell you some of the questions that helped me. Why don't you write these down on the back of the drawing.

> Has anything changed either in, or around me, over the past few years?
> How can my talents touch the world and bring me deep joy?
> What kind of person/spouse/parent/friend do I want to be?
> When it's all said and done, what is the legacy I want to leave behind?

"These questions have the power to peel back layers of life that can keep us in roles and routines we feel trapped in."

As George scribbled down the questions, Jim continued, "Sacred questions force us to look deeper into ourselves so we can identify the root of what's blocking joy and purpose in our lives. They get answered in the next phase—the *renewal phase*, but you identify them here. You will have to determine your list of sacred questions."

"Okay, Jim. I see the next step is where renewal actually happens. Is that true?" George asked.

"Yes. The renewal phase is where the action is. The formula I used to find renewal is simple to understand, but takes some thought and work. Let's look at it here."

Jim paused, tapped on the drawing, and allowed George time to read the *Traction Formula* in the following four words.

Introspection + Redirection + Action = Traction

"Traction. I'd like some of that right now," George bemoaned.

"It will come, George. I've discovered that courageous people don't *just* blaze the trail into a successful vocation—you've done that—they take the courageous step to blaze a trail into their own story and look more closely at it. Doing this gets ramped up in the renewal process. Renewal will be the by-product of the work done here. Let me explain.

"In this phase you deliberately inspect your life. You examine what's going on in and around you. You allow curiosity to become your friend. You step back and work through your sacred questions. You pay attention to how you feel and what is preoccupying your thoughts. It's here you get clear concerning the type of person you want to be *and* the kind of life you want to live. *Introspection* will help you identify the aspects of your life where you need to make changes.

"As you begin to identify the adjustments that need to be made, the renewal process will call for areas of your life to be redirected. Imagine driving a car and you realize you are heading in the wrong direction. You are driving east and you should be heading west. It's not enough to recognize you are going in the wrong direction. It's not enough to just slow down, and it's not enough to stop the car. You must turn the car around and point it in a different direction. That is the shift *redirection* calls for. You cannot remain on the same path going in the same direction, at the same speed. The direction, the road, and even the pace at which you are going will likely need to change. It's unleashing your will on an area of life and creating a new speed, a new destination, and a new compass setting."

"Now once you have pointed your car in the right direction, you must put your foot on the gas pedal and move. That's what *action* is about. You have come to the realization things aren't right—you've decided on a new direction. Now you take specific actions that will get you there. Working the formula will result in the needed *traction* to move you down the road toward life, joy, and renewal."

Jim noticed George sink back into his seat so he asked, "What do you think about this so far?"

"To be honest I think I have known for a while I'm heading in the wrong direction, but all I've done is take my foot off the gas. That's not going to solve things."

"No, I'm afraid it's not, but it happens all the time. People headed in the wrong direction have a tendency to disengage rather than redirect or take action. Rather than pull back and curse how you are feeling, what would happen if you used this season to rethink the direction of where you want to go from here? Finding traction is a process that will demand gut-level honesty, openness to seeking counsel from people wiser than you, and a willingness to educate yourself on the issue of renewal. The process I went through didn't just help me survive that difficult time, it taught me how to continually renew myself so I could live each day with a whole heart," Jim explained.

People headed in the wrong direction have a tendency to disengage rather than redirect or take action.

"In this moment, it's hard to believe I could find a fresh sense of renewal given what I'm feeling right now," George admitted.

"Here's the cool thing, George, once you do the work of renewal, you will have a wisdom that guides you so you can discover your best life. The wisdom I gained through the renewal process was priceless. I relearned that life is not about shutting down, but entering each day as a grateful learner. It's not about complaining about my life circumstances, but growing. And it's not about getting all I can get, but generosity. This kind of wisdom serves me every day. So, the accumulated lessons, the regenerative practices you'll integrate through the process, and the clarity you will gain concerning the life you want to live, will change you for the rest of your life."

George sat back and crossed his arms. As he was processing all Jim had just shared, his phone buzzed. He glanced down and noticed two missed calls along with a text from Anne. The words about stopped George's heart.

> Trying to call you. Patty has been in an accident and taken to the hospital. Headed that way. Call me!

George stood up as he reread the text.

"What's the matter?"

"Jim, I have to go. My assistant has been in an accident. I'm sorry to do this, but I need to get to the hospital," George maintained eye contact with Jim as he quickly stuffed the paper Jim gave him in his pocket with one hand and searched for his car keys with the other.

Jim stood up fumbling to help George collect his jacket, and asked, "Can I drive you? What can I do?"

"No, let me find out what's going on. I'll call you later and give you the details once I know something. Thanks for this time, Jim. It's been great to talk like this, but I've got to go."

As George hurried out the front door of the coffee shop, Jim couldn't help but wonder if the sirens they heard earlier had been heading to the scene of Patty's accident.

ER

George ran his second STOP sign in less than a month when he barreled through the intersection between visitor parking and the emergency room entrance. The car bucked and rocked as the right front tire rode up onto the curb. George slammed the brakes, and parked illegally in the fire lane in front of the emergency room entrance. As he swung his door open, his foot hit the ground before the car came to rest. If Officer Bradley showed up, George didn't care.

He could barely breathe as he considered the ramifications of what was happening. George sprinted through the emergency room doors, narrowly missing an elderly lady in a wheelchair being pushed by a woman who looked to be an EMT. He turned and yelled, "Excuse me!" to the lady as he made his way to the nurses' station.

Catching his breath, he said, "I'm looking for Patty Porter. She was in a car accident, and I was told she was brought here."

"Are you family?" asked the nurse on duty.

"No, I'm her boss," George said in a frantic tone. As the words came out of his mouth he realized how insensitive it must have sounded. "We've worked together for a long time, she is practically family," George corrected himself.

Recognizing George's desperation, the nurse tried to calm him with, "She is with the doctor and being treated right now. There are a few people in the waiting room down the hall on the left. You may join them if you would like."

George turned in the direction the nurse pointed and saw a group of familiar faces standing just outside a doorway about fifty feet up the hall. He soon found out they were in the hall because they couldn't all fit in the waiting room. There were already eleven people gathered, and the accident had happened less than an hour earlier. Within another twenty minutes there were thirty-eight others, more than half of whom George did not know.

As George entered half-running, he quickly spotted Anne sitting between Paul Porter and a local florist whose name George couldn't remember. Paul was slumped over, head hanging low between his shoulders, his elbows resting on his knees, and his hands clasped in front of him. Anne was sitting next to him, her right hand on his shoulder, as she looked up and saw George.

Anne stood and hugged George tightly before leading him back out the door.

"Oh, George. It's just awful," she whispered as they entered the hallway.

"What happened?" he asked.

"Patty was on her way to the bank when an SUV ran a STOP sign and hit her on the driver's side. We haven't been told the extent of the injuries. She's in surgery is all we know. Paul says the doctor will update us as soon as they know something."

As the reality of the situation set in, George and Anne walked back into the waiting room. Anne returned to her seat while George knelt down in front of Paul's chair and put his hand on Paul's knee. "I'm so sorry, Paul, but hang in there, Patty's a fighter. It will be okay. She's in good hands." George's words sounded hollow, but there was nothing else to say. All any of them could do was wait.

Over the next hour all of the friends and family who had gathered took turns telling story after story of how Patty had affected them. Their stories told of meals prepared and delivered, long supportive conversations in moments of great sorrow, and money given without question in times of need. One woman admitted she had been in an abusive marriage and that it was Patty who had opened her home to her and her one-year-old son. She said Patty had literally saved her life.

Over the next hour all of the friends and family who had gathered took turns telling story after story of how Patty had affected them.

When a doctor finally came out, the solemn look on his face was evident to all. He slowly looked around the room and thanked everyone for their patience before asking if he could speak with immediate family. As Paul stood up and walked toward the doctor, he glanced back at Anne and George and gave a nod of desperation indicating they should join him. The doctor led the three into a small room down the hall, quietly shutting the door behind them. They were rocked by his words, "The accident has left Mrs. Porter with severe swelling on the base of her brain. She is currently in surgery with

Dr. Jenkins, the best brain surgeon in the region. She specializes in trauma situations like this one, but I'll be honest, things are very critical. We need to get the swelling under control to give her the best chance to survive. This was a very severe accident."

The words hit the trio like the blunt face of a sledgehammer. Paul sat down and began to sob as the realization set in that he could lose his wife of nearly four decades.

George felt numb as he sensed Anne's hand touch his elbow from behind. He thought to himself, *How can this be happening?*

Daisies

It was not until well into the evening that Patty was moved from recovery to the intensive care unit. The surgery had been successful, but her condition was still critical and she remained in a coma.

The crowd from earlier in the day had dispersed, leaving George, Anne, and Paul to stay the night. Paul remained with Patty while George and Anne attempted to sleep in a couple of wooden waiting room chairs covered with pink vinyl. By morning Patty was allowed two visitors at a time, so the plan was for George and Anne to rotate in and out, allowing Paul to stay by her side. Anne went back first.

George was sitting alone in the ICU waiting room anticipating his turn when he heard the words, "How's Patty?"

He looked up from the crinkled drawing in his hand and saw Jim Clarke walking through the doorway holding a bouquet of daisies.

"I finished my meetings late last night and thought I would stop by and check on her before heading back home."

"You didn't have to come by here," George stood up, reaching out to shake Jim's hand. "But I'm glad you did. Anne and Patty's husband, Paul, are back with her. She is in a coma. The doc says the next twenty-four hours are critical," George informed Jim with a clear note of worry in his voice.

"I'm so sorry, George. "Is there anything I can do for you guys while you wait?"

"We're all doing as well as we can at this point. There's just a lot of waiting to do right now. As I was sitting here I pulled out your drawing. I've been thinking about it and our conversation yesterday morning. I'm sorry we didn't get to talk about your plans to expand the business."

"No worries. We can connect again later on that," Jim said as he sat down in a waiting room chair across from George. "I'm glad to see you reflecting on the formula."

"The more I look at it, the more it makes sense to me. No wonder I've been so unfulfilled and directionless. Clearly, I'm stuck."

"Say more," Jim replied.

"Well, do you remember how you asked me why I'm not happy?" George paused. "That has been in the back of my mind since you said it. You were right. I always dreamed of being successful in my career, calling the shots at a bank, having financial freedom, and even making a difference. And now here I sit—check, check, check, check—on all four, and yet, to use your word, I'm still miserable."

"I lost my perspective and forgot about the
importance of adding value to others."

"Keep going," Jim encouraged.

"I think the timing of our meeting and getting this drawing from you, along with being faced with the possibility of losing Patty—and the reminder of just how fleeting and precious life is, has pushed me to really look at my life and the choices I am making. Somehow I lost my perspective and forgot about the importance of adding value to others. When I was truly the happiest, helping people with my banking talents was my priority. Patty never lost sight of what mattered. Recently, I clearly have."

"My friend, you are headed in the right direction and I believe you are on the cusp of renewal," Jim said admiringly.

"Why do you say that?"

"Look at the formula again."

George looked down at the now creased paper.

Jim recited the traction formula to George, "Introspection + Redirection + Action = Traction. You are in the midst of a hurricane of introspection, and that's good. It's not possible for a person to get to renewal without it. Almost like an addict has to admit he has a problem before he can make any progress on his recovery, taking the time to think deeply about where you are and admitting you are at a STOP sign . . . stuck . . . however you want to say it, is step one. You're on your way, George."

George slightly grinned, "Being stuck makes me on my way?"

"That's right!" chuckled Jim.

"Beautiful!" George responded with a bigger grin.

The bit of laughter felt great. It had been a pressure-cooked twenty-four hours in the midst of months of malaise for George. Jim's words now resonated even more than they had the day before. George felt a ray of hope with the thought that he was heading in the right direction and the prospect of being able to share with Patty that he was sorry for how his situation had affected his work. If only she could pull through.

As their conversation was ending, George glanced to the door of the ICU waiting room. In hurried Patty's daughters, Faith and Sarah Porter.

"We just landed on the red-eye. I was out in California visiting Faith," Sarah said, almost out of breath. "How is Mom?"

George stood to hug the young women he had known since they were girls. He filled them in on the details of the accident and their mom's current condition before telling them they could go and relieve their dad and Anne.

Jim said, "I'm going to head out so you can walk them back, George. I'll check in on you all in a couple of days. Let me know if you need anything."

"I will, and thanks again for stopping by. I'm truly grateful for all you have done for me, and I know Paul and Patty will appreciate your thoughtfulness. She will love the daisies."

Gone Missing

After leaving the girls to sit with Patty, an exhausted George, Anne, and Paul returned to the waiting room. Anne urged the men to go and get some breakfast, assuring them she would let them know if anything changed. Both men agreed and reached for their phones as they exited the waiting room.

George and Paul both ordered pancakes and coffee in the hospital cafeteria. Neither ate very much, but the break from the hours of helplessly waiting was much needed.

"I'm so sorry, Paul." George said noticing that Paul was blankly staring out the cafeteria window.

"Me too, George," Paul responded. "Part of me thinks this isn't really happening, but then I think about Patty's gift statement."

"Her gift statement?"

"Yeah. She reminds me every morning that each day is a gift and I should make the most of it. That's the last thing she said yesterday morning before she kissed me on the cheek and walked out the door."

"She says the same thing at the bank all the time, minus the kiss," George smiled, attempting to lighten things a bit.

"Patty loves working at the bank. It brings her joy to have a place to feel like she is making a difference in the community and in the lives of people. I've never heard her complain one time about her job. She loves it."

"That's pretty obvious," George acknowledged. "She's amazing."

"Frankly, she has been a bit concerned about you lately. She says the old George has gone missing."

"I know. I've lost my way a bit. Patty has been on my case about it."

"Honesty is her MO," Paul said, now the one smiling.

"I often wonder how I have kept her with us at the bank for so long," George said.

"I wonder the same thing—about me, not you," Paul replied reminiscing over thirty-eight years of marriage.

"George, the bank is more than a job for Patty. It has been her passion. She had several offers through the years to leave the bank; some would even have been much better financially. But she always told me she couldn't bear the thought of you trying to help all those people without someone helping you."

Paul's words rocked George. He had assumed that was the case, but to hear it directly from Paul caused him to tear up. George pushed away his pancakes and remained silent.

Each day is a gift and you should make the
most of it.

"After Faith and Sarah were school age, Patty wanted to get a job where she could work with 'big people,' as she called them—the grown-ups. When you first hired her, she was beside herself. I've never seen someone so excited. All she talked about was the opportunity to work with such a great team. We're not that much older than you guys, but I think Patty saw you as the son we never had. She would come home and tell me every time you did something great. 'He's making a difference and changing our small part of the world,' she would say. She literally cried the night you offered her the opportunity to come over with you when the new bank started. She said she never dreamed she would have the chance to serve our community in such a tangible way. After a year or so we rarely went out without people coming up to us and thanking her for being such a good friend. The bank became her platform to bless people."

George sat back, taking in all he was hearing. "Patty never lost sight of what matters. I only wish I hadn't."

"She has never lost faith in you, George."

The two men lingered over the coffee until it was stone cold. Finally, George urged Paul to go home and take a break. "I'll stay with the girls until you get back. Go get some rest and a hot shower. It's going to be a long week."

Paul agreed and they exited the cafeteria. George caught the elevator to the seventh floor, where he encouraged Anne to also take a break. He would take the afternoon shift with Sarah and Faith, when he would discover he was not the only one who was feeling stuck.

Everyone Needs Traction

George met Faith and Sarah walking out of the double doors from the ICU. He was encouraged by the news that the doctor had stopped by, and she had told them their mom was making progress. "While technically we still would call it a coma, we are keeping her sedated to give her the opportunity to recover. The swelling is going down, and I'm hoping she will be awake within the next twenty-four hours. The MRI shows no bleeding and no long-term damage," were the doctor's words.

The sisters led the way into the waiting room where the three of them remained for the rest of the morning giving them a chance to catch up on their lives, and giving Patty the chance to rest. After calling Paul and sharing the news with him, they sat with a clear sense of relief.

"Mr. Johnson, who was that man who was with you early this morning? The guy with the daisies?" Faith asked.

"Please, call me George. Mr. Johnson makes me feel old."

"You are old," Sarah teased. "You're going to be the big 5-0 in a couple of years, aren't you?"

"Almost three years, thank you very much. I'm holding on hard to forty-seven, which technically means I'm still in my mid-forties." George grinned, trying to convince himself. Continuing, he said, "That was Jim Clarke. He has become a new friend of our family during this past year. He helped Mark navigate his senior year of college and get clear on his future. He's sort of a guru when it comes to helping people who are stuck."

"I can't believe Mark graduated. It seems like just yesterday that Faith and I were babysitting for you guys."

"Remember the time Mark ate an entire package of Oreos?" Faith revealed.

The three laughed as they reminisced over their history together as families and Mark's sneaky love of sweets.

"That was nice of him," Sarah said oddly.

George and Faith looked at her seeking to understand.

"For Mr. Clarke to come by," Sarah pieced together her thought.

"He's a really good man," George acknowledged.

"I could use one," Faith said.

"A really good man?" questioned her sister.

"Well, one of those too," Faith laughed. "But I was referring to a guru."

"Why would you need a guru, Faith? You are the guru. You have always given me good counsel in tough moments," Sarah said admiringly to her older sister.

George smiled as he listened to Sarah's words. He turned to Faith and stated, "Your mom told me you were promoted to chief marketing officer at the beginning of the year. Pretty impressive for someone in her mid-thirties."

"I'm thirty-three, which technically I'm telling myself is still my early thirties," Faith said winking at George.

Sarah and George both laughed and breathed a little lighter.

Faith continued, "Don't get me wrong, the job is great. But . . ."

"But what?" Sarah invited.

"But it just feels like something is missing," Faith admitted.

"What's missing? You have it all. An incredible condo overlooking the bay, you can come and go as you please, and you make more money than you can spend. I'd say you are living your dream," Sarah challenged with a tinge of envy.

"You are the one living the dream," Faith countered. "You have an amazing husband who thinks you created the moon before you hung it and the two cutest little guys on the planet."

"Sounds like you both are living the dream, just different ones," George reminded them.

Tears began to roll down Sarah's face. George assumed it was because of Patty and attempted to reassure her of the doctor's words. It quickly became apparent the tears were only partially for Patty. Like her sister, Sarah was also feeling stuck. She began to open up about how she felt her dreams were on hold, admitting there were even times when she resented her duties as a wife and mom.

Faith was stunned to hear her little sister acknowledge that her fairy-tale life was less than ideal. "I just assumed everything was perfect. Why didn't you say something?"

"I just flew across the country to visit you. Didn't that tell you something?" Sarah half-laughed through the tears.

George handed her a tissue from a box on the corner table. Faith, who was sitting across, moved out of her chair and hugged her younger sister. To give the girls space, George walked out to an alcove just outside the waiting room door where there was a coffee station. He brought in three cups to find the girls back in their chairs talking about their lives. For the next hour George had a front-row seat to an honest and revealing conversation between the Porter girls. As George listened it became obvious to him that even though they were different ages they all had something in common—each of them felt stuck.

Faith shared how lonely she was at times. Though her job was fulfilling, her personal life was on hold, with no prospects of a meaningful relationship. She revealed she still hoped to have children and yet wondered if it would ever happen.

Sarah was up to her eyeballs in diapers and messy spills. She longed to give more time to her passion for food. She dreamed of a catering business and an event center where she could create experiences for the people of her community.

Faith tried to convince Sarah to go after her dream. Sarah assured Faith that she was amazing and that she could have any guy she wanted if she would simply slow down and make time for it. It was evident that both girls secretly longed to swap places with the other.

Finally, George found the courage to join the conversation. "Me too."

"Excuse me?" Sarah questioned.

"I guess I can relate to how you girls are feeling," George revealed. "The fact is, one of the reasons Jim was in town the past couple of days was to meet with me about some things that have been going on in my life."

"Things going on in your life, Mr. Johnson? What things? What do you mean?" Faith questioned.

Following the example of these two honest and transparent young women, George decided to bear his soul. He told them about his challenges at work, the struggle of letting Mark go, and the feeling that he was spinning his wheels. He was surprised that it didn't feel awkward. Perhaps recognizing the girls were similarly struggling made it easier to talk, or maybe it was the shared vulnerability they all felt in the aftermath of Patty's accident. Whatever it was, George explained why he was feeling stuck. As he finished telling the girls some of his story he reached into his pocket and pulled out the paper with Jim's traction formula.

As he stared at it Sarah asked, "What's on that paper?"

"It's what Jim shared with me yesterday morning during our breakfast. It's his wisdom on how to get unstuck in life."

"What does it say?" Faith asked.

"To be honest, I'm just starting to digest it. I received news of your mom's accident right in the middle of our conversation, so we had to cut it short. But, he certainly gave me enough to think about."

"So, let's hear it. What did he tell you? The Porter girls want to know. I feel stuck watching my business dream slip away and a cute husband for Faith might be hanging in the balance," Sarah responded, ribbing her sister.

"Well, according to Jim, there appear to be three steps to gaining the traction needed to get out of stuck places. His traction formula reads like this:

"Introspection + Redirection + Action = Traction."

"Cool. It actually rhymes," Faith blurted out.

"I know. I know it does," George replied.

"But the more I think about it, the more sense it makes. If this formula is true then it should apply not just to me in my middle forties, but to you, Faith, in your early thirties, and to you, Sarah, in your late twenties. It should touch every life at every phase and every age. It should help a teenager who feels lonely. It should help someone who is retried and wondering if he still has meaning. And if this formula became like a mental compass, it should certainly help us daily stay out of the ruts that life offers."

"If this formula is true then it should apply not just
to me ... it should touch every life at every phase
and every age."

"Okay, if Sarah and I are to get needed traction it looks like introspection is step one."

"That's what Jim said and it's what we have done over this past hour as we have each discussed our lives. You two both looked at your life stories and identified what is currently frustrating you. The formula says we must reflect long enough to decide on the life we want and ask ourselves if that is the life we currently have. Then, if we aren't headed in the right direction, we need to redirect. Finally, we must take small action steps to head in the desired direction. When we do, momentum begins and traction is experienced. At least that's how I understand it."

As George was finishing his thought a nurse walked into the waiting room and interrupted.

"Excuse me, I came on shift thirty minutes ago. Are you Patty Porter's children?"

Faith responded that she and Sarah were Patty's daughters and that George was a close family friend.

"Well, you won't believe this, but your mother opened her eyes ten minutes ago. I stopped in to check her vitals and she squeezed my hand and said she was thirsty. It looks like she is having a faster recovery than expected; she must be a strong woman. The doctor is in with her now. If things check out the two of you should be able to talk to her within the hour."

Both girls stood speechless. They thanked the nurse, turned, and hugged each other. Then George got the hug of his lifetime. The nurse said she would be back as soon as it was okay for them to see their mom. George told Faith to call her dad and that he would call Anne to let her know.

Once the calls were made the three of them sat together quietly for a few moments. George broke the silence. "Can you believe the nurse thought I was your brother?"

The three of them laughed together.

"How was your dad?"

Faith replied, "He broke down and cried on the phone. He's on his way back."

With gratefulness in her voice, Sarah said, "George, thanks for being here for Mom, Dad, Faith, and myself and for caring for us girls while we were growing up. You and Anne are like family. We also appreciate you for listening to us this morning and for sharing with us about your own struggles. For what it's worth, it's pretty cool to have someone further up the road that we can lean into."

"Thanks. That's what big brothers are for," George responded with a grin.

"After we see Mom, why don't you head home, check on Anne and get a little rest. It will give Faith and me some time with her and a chance to process everything that's going on, including Jim's wisdom on how to find traction."

"Sounds like a plan," George answered. "And thanks for your generous words. Just know I'm in the middle of getting unstuck too. So, let's move ahead together. If I can ever help either of you, please just let me know. But for now, let's do everything we can to get your mom healed and healthy."

Relief

On Wednesday morning, Patty was more alert and eager to be moved to a regular room. She got her wish and landed in room 421. Faith and Sarah had stayed with Paul through the night, and they were all exhausted.

When George arrived he encouraged Paul and the girls to take a break. Sarah decided to stay while Paul and Faith agreed to go home for a few hours.

Patty dozed for the first hour before awaking to discover George sitting in a chair in the corner reading a magazine and Sarah napping in an elongated sleeper chair.

George pulled his chair over to Patty's bedside.

"Good morning, young lady."

"Hey, stranger. Did you miss me at the bank so much that you had to come check on me again today?"

"Something like that. I'm glad to see you feeling better."

"How's Paul?" Patty asked, now wide awake.

Patty somehow found the strength to become the teacher in a class she had never even taken.

"He's hanging in there but pretty worried about his sweetheart. He and Faith went home for a break. He said to tell you he will be back in a couple hours. I think he's determined to sleep in this chair tonight. It looks like you're stuck with him." George smiled tapping his hands on the arms of the chair. "The real question is how are you doing?"

Glancing her eyes up at the bandage wrapped around her head, Patty replied, "I've got some mending to do, but other than that, I'm doing fine."

George laughed at her tenacity.

"How did your meeting go?" she asked.

"My meeting?'

"Your meeting with Jim Clarke on Monday morning. Did he get you straightened out?" Patty teased with a chuckle.

Shocked that Patty could remember anything, much less his meeting with Jim, George replied, "Truthfully, I've been thinking about my time with him for the past couple of days."

George pulled Jim's diagram from his pocket and held it up for Patty to see. "He drew this for me."

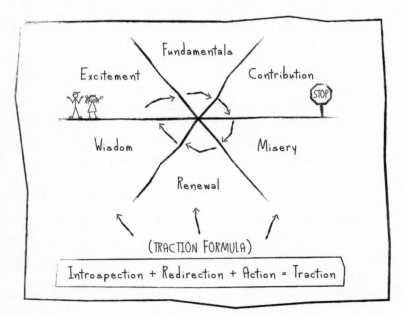

Patty carefully studied the six phases before looking back at George and intuitively stating, "Let me guess. This big STOP sign has something to do with your situation."

The conversation that took place over the next hour was life changing for George. Patty somehow became the teacher in a class she had never even taken. Using Jim's formula, and finding enough strength and stamina to talk, she skillfully redirected George toward renewal.

"Remember who you are and why you do what you do," was the phrase she repeated four times before they were done. When George left he knew he needed to redirect his future back toward the core of his past. The thought brought a hint of relief.

Reflection

When George arrived home that night Anne was napping on the couch. She had left him a turkey sandwich in the refrigerator, and he took it out on the covered porch overlooking the backyard. The summer breeze had cooled, and it was a peaceful evening. George finished the sandwich and lay down in the hammock that stretched between two porch posts. In less than a minute he was asleep.

At midnight George was awakened by the sound of a barking dog. As he opened his eyes, a fog surrounded his mind and heart.

He got up out of the hammock and went back into the house. He noticed Anne had relocated from the sofa to the bed. Although still tired, George was no longer sleepy. He walked into his home office and sat in the comfortable leather chair at his antique desk. He pulled out the diagram Jim Clarke had drawn and began to contemplate it again.

As he considered each of the six phases, he quickly categorized the various people he had met throughout his week to the stages in the top half of the diagram. A young nurse named Joy represented phase 1, the *excitement phase*. Her attitude and energy in the ICU had been off the charts. It had been years since George had felt anything close to what Joy had demonstrated. However, as he reflected, he was forced to admit even all these years later,

Patty had somehow maintained her excitement and passion for what she did.

As he looked beneath it he read the word *misery*. A word that accurately summed up all he was feeling.

Phase 2 was the *fundamentals phase*. He thought of all the doctors who had cared for Patty and the high price each must have paid to go through medical school, to spend endless hours away from their families learning so they could help others. He was thankful for all the teachers who had mentored each doctor, and the families who loved and supported their passions. George reflected on the first decade of his career. His years at Conroy Investment had been ones of tremendous growth. He had learned the fundamentals of banking thanks to his mentor Carlton Conroy. Carlton was the owner of the firm and had taken George under his wing. For months George had sat in on every meeting Carlton would allow him to attend. He took copious notes and reviewed them every night. Growth defined him during that time.

Phase 3, represented in the third pie slice of the drawing, was the *contribution phase*. Jim had said at Monday's breakfast that in this phase, "competence has been achieved, and your talent is touching the world in a productive way." George pictured Patty at the bank always making a difference and adding value to everyone she touched. He, too, had once been motivated by contribution. Coupled with the fact that he knew as much about banking as anyone in the region, George and Patty had been a powerful team. But now Patty was in the hospital, and he was stuck at the STOP sign.

The good old STOP sign. There it was again square in George's path. It felt like a barrier between where he was and where he wanted to go until he looked beneath it and realized he was already in phase four: *misery.* A word that accurately summed up all he had been feeling. Looking back, George realized there had been many indicators over the past few years that he was approaching a vocational STOP sign. A lack of motivation, disengagement, and despair all had their tentacles entwined around his career. He truly dreamed of somehow freshly reengaging his work and rediscovering joy in what he once loved to do. But it was undeniable, although he once loved banking—now he found himself in a job that no longer felt meaningful.

Yet Patty had somehow maintained her passion for what she did. She brought joy and excitement into the bank every day. George had watched her continue to grow as an employee, but more important, as a person. It appeared she had skipped the misery phase. She saw every day as a gift and simply made the most of it.

Jim Clarke had encouraged introspection as the beginning place of gaining traction in the process of renewal. Patty, it seemed, understood the need for redirection as well when she said, "Remember who you are and why you do what you do." INTROSPECTION + REDIRECTION.

Is it possible for me to regain perspective and find renewal? It was the last thought he had before he leaned back in his chair and fell into a deep sleep.

It's in the Doing

The next afternoon, George's phone vibrated as he pulled out of the hospital parking lot. Caller ID revealed it to be Jim Clarke.

"Jim. What's up?"

"Hey, George. Just calling to check in and see how Patty is doing. Have you had a chance to see her yet today?"

"As a matter of fact I'm just leaving the hospital. Had another great chat with her today."

"How is she?"

"She has a bunch of bruising and small cuts from the shattered windshield. Truthfully, she looks like she was in a bar fight and lost. I can't imagine how much pain she must be in, but true to form, the woman is not a complainer. Unbelievable! The doctor says it is going to take a while to heal up, but she should make a full recovery," George said with happiness.

"So, you had a good visit?"

"Really good. She asked me how I heard about the accident. I told her we were meeting at a coffee shop and news came via a text from Anne. I also mentioned that the first responders heading to her accident drove right by us. I let her know we had no idea they were on the way to the accident she was in. Patty said she can't wait to find out who those people were and thank them. She was unconscious when they transported her from the accident site to the hospital. She's already assigned Paul the task of getting their names and numbers. Also, don't be surprised if she sends you flowers for bringing her flowers. You gotta love her."

"Yeah, she sounds like someone very special."

"I also mentioned that you wanted to discuss a business expansion idea. But I told her we got kind of side-tracked talking about me."

"You told her about that?"

"Yes. She knows I've been feeling disconnected for a while. She was thrilled I finally had the chance to talk with someone about it. I even pulled out your drawing and gave her the overview of the six-phase construct and walked her though the traction formula."

"Really? What was her response?"

"First thing she said was to tell you to take an art class."

"Very funny! The pain meds must have been affecting her vision. That drawing is a masterpiece."

Both men laughed out loud.

"Remember who you are and why you do what you do."

"Seriously, she found it really interesting and agreed I'm probably somewhere between *misery* and *renewal* in the process. She thinks the traction formula is spot on, especially the *redirection* part. Then she said some things I needed to hear. I'll tell you, the woman is relentless. Even while fully medicated she was able to help me gain more perspective."

"Amazing," Jim acknowledged.

"Yep. She was really candid. At one point in our conversation she said, 'George, you have to make some decisions concerning who you are going to be from here on out. These days we have at the bank are limited.' She kept reminding me of who I *used* to be by repeating the phrase, 'Remember who you are and why you do what you do.'"

"Way to go, Patty. I love that she got after the boss a little," Jim commented.

"I know," George said with a chuckle. "I listened to what she was saying and she's right. I can see how my direction needs to change with Anne, my sons, the people at the bank, and my future."

"George, as important as *redirection* is in the renewal process, things won't change until you take *action*. You can introspect and redirect all you want, but remember, you have to have a bias for action. Don't forget that it's in the doing—taking the right steps, treating others differently, making the apologies, adjusting your behavior—in these actions that real renewal is birthed. So, I want you to begin to consider what specific actions you need to take. Each action completed will give you additional traction as you move toward renewal. The traction you get isn't renewal; it simply generates movement in that direction. It's as if you are planting seeds for renewal and the action you take is like watering those seeds. Pretty soon a momentum will emerge and renewal will be experienced. As we talked about before, renewal is a by-product of introspection, redirection, and action."

"I see that now. I will think seriously about what the next right action is and commit to doing it. Thanks for the call, Jim. Let's stay in touch over this next week."

"Sounds great, George."

Both men clicked off the call as George came to a STOP sign. A left would take him toward home. George turned to the right.

Action

As his car turned onto the highway, headed in the opposite direction of his home, George thought, *There is no time like the present to take action.* Within minutes he was sitting in Morton Frazier's driveway. Morton was painting the handrails on his front porch. Lost in his work, he didn't even notice George had pulled up.

George sat in his car for a minute and watched as Morton carefully brushed each picket. He looked like an artist working on a canvas. The attention to detail caught George off guard. It was a beautiful porch. George knew Morton had built the porch because Morton had taken out a construction loan from the bank for the remodel. Morton had been so excited about adding onto the house. George remembered thinking back then, *Why would anyone want to spend their free time doing a construction project on their home?* But now, George was staring at one of the nicest-looking entryways in town. Morton was truly a master carpenter.

As he opened the car door, Morton looked up. When he saw George, he immediately laid down the brush and hurried over to him.

"George! What a nice surprise. How's Patty doing? We were so sorry to hear about the accident," Morton said as he offered George a warm handshake. "Margaret and I are going over to visit this evening. Sounds like it was a really bad wreck."

"It was, but she's doing better every day. They may even let her go home by the weekend," George replied.

Morton wiped his brow with a blue bandanna. "How's Paul doing?" he asked.

"He's hanging in there, but he's still pretty distraught," George responded.

"I'd imagine so. Patty is a good one."

"You got that right."

There is no time like the present to take action.

"What brings you by this afternoon, George?" Morton asked, adjusting his hat higher on his head.

I need to clear my conscience felt a bit direct, so George resisted saying that.

"I just wanted to stop by and thank you for the great job you did on the bank. The gutters look wonderful."

"Thanks, George. I appreciate that. But did you really stop by to tell me the gutters look great?"

"Actually, Morton, I want to apologize. I haven't been as good a friend as I need to be. Patty told me about how challenging it has been for you and Paula lately, and truthfully, I was completely unaware of the situation."

"Thank you, George. That means a lot coming from you," Morton responded, recognizing the humility the bank president was demonstrating.

"I mean it, Morton. I really am sorry I haven't been a better friend. If there is anything Anne and I can do for your family, give us a call."

"Thanks. We are doing fine right now, but I really appreciate the offer."

"The porch is looking great," George said as he reached to shake Morton's hand once again.

Morton instead embraced his friend. As the two men hugged, George felt a sense of relief. He knew that if Patty were watching she would have been pleased.

As he drove home, George felt remarkably relieved. As he looked into the rearview mirror, it was as if he had somehow gained just a bit of distance from misery. On the half-hour drive home, he called both of his sons and had a heartfelt conversation with each. He affirmed his love for them and reminded them of what a gift they were to him and Anne. He pulled into the market a mile from his neighborhood and bought an arrangement of tulips, Anne's favorite. Moments later he found her in the kitchen about to make dinner for the two of them.

"Hold everything, beautiful lady. How would you like to go out to dinner?" George asked as he revealed the tulips he was concealing behind his back.

"Are you asking me for a date, Mr. Johnson?"

"I am indeed, Mrs. Johnson. But first I have something I need to say."

Over the next few minutes George opened his heart to his wife. With the resolute intensity of a changed man, George proclaimed, "I've been doing some thinking and some deciding over the past few days. It's time for me to do a few things differently. I have reassessed who I've been recently, and I'm not happy with that person. As a step toward change, I have resolved to take action and apologize to those I've hurt or neglected or shut out, and that starts with you. I'm sorry . . ."

George had to pause and wait for a wave of emotion to pass. "I'm sorry for the way I've been recently. You are my most precious gift, and I will treat you accordingly from this day forward. Will you please forgive me?"

Anne smiled as tears filled her eyes. "You're forgiven, Mr. Johnson. How could I say no to a dashing bank president with an arm full of tulips?"

Renewal

Three weeks after the day of Patty's accident, Jim returned to the coffee shop where he and George first had breakfast. George was already there, having claimed the same table by the window. Jim grabbed a mocha latte and joined him. As Jim sat down, he noticed George was writing notes on the crinkled page that held the drawing Jim had scribbled at their meeting.

"Good morning, my friend," Jim offered.

"Great to see you," George replied.

"I see you are jotting down some thoughts. It's nice to see you still have the drawing."

"Jim, I've been living on this page since you sketched it out. I've been looking at life through the lens of this construct. The longer I think about what it communicates, the more sense it makes. Hopefully we can talk about phases 5 and 6—*renewal* and *wisdom*.

"We can, George. But before we do, how's Patty?"

"She's amazing—making progress every day. Still using a cane for now, but her spirits are as strong as ever. She told me yesterday she is going to drop by the bank and surprise everyone in a few days."

"How long until she comes back to work?"

"It looks like it will be a few more weeks, but with her, you never can tell. The woman defies all the odds," George replied with a smile.

"So tell me about you. How's the *action* step been going?"

"I think I have had a breakthrough. I have to admit, I feel more alive than I have in several years. I never would have believed it, but I think the formula works."

"That's great, George. I know how you feel, and I'm really happy for you."

"Part of me is afraid this is too good to be true. I keep wondering how long this will last."

"Well, I guess there are no guarantees, but I suspect you won't be getting stuck again anytime soon. And if by some chance you do stall, now you will know the way back to traction."

Without looking at the paper, George acknowledged, "Introspection + Redirection + Action—will give me traction and keep me moving toward renewal."

"You got it, pal. The beauty is, you now have the process to continually experience renewal."

"What do you mean?" George inquired sensing the answer was more than the simple formula.

"Renewal is an ongoing process that never ends. It is about continuously assessing, adjusting, and redirecting your life. It's about choosing to write a new and fresh story moving forward. The steps toward renewal—the formula—are simple to understand, but also challenging to continually live out."

"Can you explain a little further?" George prompted.

"Well, there really are no guarantees. What got you stuck in the first place can certainly derail you again. When you live today fully aware that life is about learning, growing, and generosity, that doesn't mean you will live like that tomorrow. Renewal is a daily choice. On any given day you can slide backward into selfishness, making comfort and ease your life priorities. I hope that will never happen to you again, but it could if you fail to spend time on introspection and continual redirection. If you stop walking toward, to use Patty's words, 'who you are and why you do what you do,' you can end up, as you know, in a bad place. And there are no shortcuts to achieving the life you want. This stuff requires continual work."

> "Renewal is all about redirecting your life. It's about choosing to write a new and fresh story moving forward."

"Are there any secrets to staying on course?"

Jim answered, "There are a couple of action steps you can take here. The first is to create a document you can continually refer to and update. Some people call this their 'Personal Manifesto.' I don't care what you call it, just be sure to create it. This document should be the ongoing thoughts and actions of the *renewal phase* and should articulate the type of person you want to be and the sort of life you want to live. This document will out-line the new story—the best story—of you. Once the doc-ument is created, be aware that the busyness of life and the crazy pace of things can cloud your thinking. In those moments come back to the document and *redirect* toward it. You may want to adjust and update it with your latest thoughts on life. This document should include a definition of your life's purpose. Living out your purpose in an *action*-oriented way is critical for ongoing renewal. When you first draft it, you will want to review it at least every week.

He continued, "A second action step is to identify other regenerative practices and schedule them into your calendar. Activities that foster self-care are critical to the process. Everyone around you, beginning with Anne, your sons, and those at the bank, needs an ever-renewed you. You must learn to balance selflessly serving others and caring for yourself. Healthy people understand the need to keep their own heart fresh. This is vital, George. You must identify what refreshes you. Is it reading? Solitude? Music? Prayer? Journaling? Golf? Walking in nature? Recreation? You have to identify where the rhythm between the action of work and the renewal of your heart exists. What renews you now might be different than ten years ago. Make these practices personal, practical, and positive."

"Tell me about the wisdom phase," George requested.

"In the *wisdom phase* we collect life lessons and learn to live with better perspective. The drawing identifies the two lifelong works of personal development. Look at the six phases again and notice the horizontal line across the page. Imagine that line is the surface of the ocean—a waterline. That would mean the three phases on top of the line are above the waterline and the three under are below the waterline."

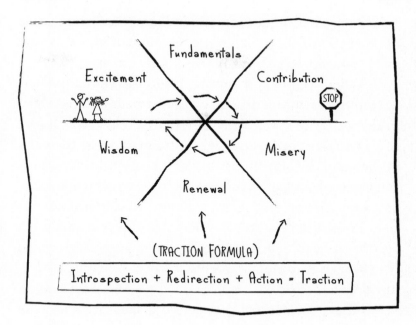

George looked at the drawing.

"The three phases above the horizontal line are about the work of the work. *Excitement—fundamentals—contribution* are about you discovering and developing yourself so you can accomplish the work with your name on it. The first half of one's life for most people is pretty much about that. We identify and prepare for the work we want and start advancing in our careers."

"The work of the HEART is what takes place below the horizontal line. *Misery—Renewal—Wisdom* are about growth, depth, character, soul, congruence, and living from your authentic self. This is what the second half of life is about. Maturity is being capable and competent above *and* authentic and integrous below the waterline. Does that make sense?"

"It does. I'm guessing you aren't saying people give up the work of the WORK in the second half of life. Is that true?" George wondered.

"That's right; we continue to do the work with our name on it. It's just that as we grow in the work of the HEART we come to our work differently. It is a critical part of human development. You may be working at the bank in the same role. But I'm guessing you are a different person given what's happened in you over the past few weeks."

George responded, "Absolutely. No question about that. I'm a different person today than I was even a week ago because of the work you've encouraged me to do beneath the waterline—the heart work. And I know I've just begun this work."

"You are different, George. I can sense it. There is a new and deeper authority to your life. Those who do the work of the heart communicate differently, love better, see more clearly, are more whole, and certainly more secure. You aren't going to forget how to be a bank president as you grow beneath the waterline in the second half of life. It's just that you are choosing to live more wholeheartedly. It feels good, doesn't it?" Jim asked.

"You told me the first time we met that I had no idea what I was missing. Well, you were right. I want to live being a great bank president *and* a person with an ever-expanding, deepening heart. That's the direction I'm heading, so thank you, Jim. I mean it. I wouldn't have gotten here without you."

"I'm so glad for you, George. I think you will find that there will be a whole new level of contribution you will make in the days ahead that will be deeper, richer, and more helpful to others because of the person you are becoming."

"I'm counting on it," George responded with hope in his voice.

After a slight pause, George turned the conversation toward Jim. "Now, enough about me. We still haven't gotten to the reason for your initial call. I want to hear about the opportunity you have to expand to a second location for The Wake Up and see if I can lend any perspective. I at least owe you that much."

"I'll tell you what. Let's put that on hold. Let's let today be about what has happened in you." Jim paused before adding, "What would you think about spending a Saturday together in a few weeks to discuss my business? I've been wanting to fish the lake over in Springfield. It's about halfway between us, and I've never fished it. My old partner Daniel just bought a little cabin over there, and I'm sure he would let us have it for a weekend. If Anne will give you a pass for a Friday night with a friend, I'll meet you at the lake and we can grill some steaks and hang out and talk business. On Saturday morning we can give the bass a go and fish till mid-afternoon. You'll be home by dinner. What do you say?"

"Are you kidding? Anne will love having me out of the house. Especially if it's time with you," George said emphatically with a laugh. "An opportunity for a regenerative activity—I'm in!"

Both men smiled and sat quietly looking out the window. Both sensed the importance of what had just happened in their conversation. Each knew that to speak any more might dishonor the moment. The true meaning of their time together and growing friendship could only be understood on the other side of words. So, they sat not saying anything, just being grateful to be friends in this moment of time. When their eyes did meet after the silence, Jim gave George a small affirming nod. George returned the gesture. In a moment neither would ever forget, both knew George had recovered his life.

Welcome Back

The grandfather clock in the corner of George's office struck 5:00 PM as he was wrapping up a meeting with a young couple who were applying for a new home loan. As George walked them to the front door, he assured them they could expect a call from him tomorrow. He smiled when he noticed Paul and Patty making their way from the parking lot to the bank's entrance.

Patty shouted, "Hey, keep that door open. We're here to rob the place."

George said with a grin, "Sorry, lady, the bank's closed. You'll have to come back tomorrow."

"Very funny, George. You better watch what you say, my cane makes a pretty good weapon."

It had been a month since the accident, and all of Patty's cuts were healed and her bruises had disappeared. She had a slight limp, but considering the severity of the crash she refused to complain. This was her first time back to the bank since the accident, and she couldn't wait to see everyone.

"Glad you two made it. Everyone is excited to see you."

As Patty navigated her way past George into the bank, she rapped him on the shin with her walking stick and whispered, "Didn't anyone ever teach you to respect your elders?"

George smiled as he locked the front door of the bank behind her.

No one knew when Patty would be strong enough to return full time as George's assistant, but the anticipation was building that it would be sooner than later. In the meantime, she wanted to come by and thank everyone for their love and support during her recovery. Her call to George earlier in the day revealed that today would be that day. After her call, George went, one by one, telling each staff member that Patty would be by at closing time. Everyone couldn't wait to see her.

Once inside the bank, it didn't take long for a line to form in front of Patty as everyone wanted to greet her personally. Leonard, a new hire at the bank, introduced himself, saying he was honored to meet a legend.

Patty responded, "Don't believe everything this bunch tells you."

Maureen set up a small table with cupcakes, punch, and coffee. She also brought out balloons she had picked up at lunch that read "Welcome Back" and "We Missed You."

George went to his office and rolled out his high-back leather chair for her, and she gladly plopped down into it. As she did, George exclaimed, "Look everyone, the queen is back on her throne and all is well once again in the kingdom!"

Everyone roared, and Patty glanced up at George and said, "My, you are doing better, aren't you?"

A couple of staff retrieved chairs from the other offices and set them so they were all facing Patty. People were invited to grab a cupcake and a drink, and then be seated.

George stood beside Patty and asked for everyone's attention. "What a great day this is. As a staff, we are like family and it's good to have the entire family back together again." He turned to Patty and said, "Welcome back, friend. This place hasn't been the same without you."

Maureen blurted out, "Amen to that!" and everyone nodded in agreement.

"Patty, while you have been away from the bank, we have all been talking about you behind your back. That's right. There has been a lot of gossip flying around this place about you. Some of it has even been positive," George said with a big grin.

The entire staff started to laugh.

"So, as a staff we wanted to take a few minutes and confess publicly what we have been saying about you privately. Everyone wants to say what they've missed about you or what they've learned from you over the years, or even, what they have learned watching you deal with your recovery. Now, I know you. You are going to want to deflect these comments and point to everyone else. We will not let you do that today. So, there is a 'No talk' rule for you while we share. Got it?"

"I don't like it, but I'll allow it," Patty responded with a frown as Paul nodded and smiled.

"Now, who wants to go first?" George asked.

Maureen volunteered. "Patty, I've had the chance to walk in your shoes this past month, and your job is even more difficult than I thought it would be. I have met a lot of the people face to face that you work with. Not every one of them was polite or even nice. This experience has awakened me to something special about you. Today, I want to thank you for your unrelenting belief in people. You see the good in everyone. Not only that, you see the good in each of us here at the bank—and specifically, in me. Thanks for suggesting to George that I could serve as an interim in your role. I have learned a lot. Now, hurry back!"

Patty started to say something, but George intercepted her and said, "Patty! No responding until we have all had a chance to share."

Marcus, the bank's IT specialist, stood up next. "Patty, I want to thank you for bringing life to this place every day. So many people walk in here busy or in a hurry or even frowning, yet their attitudes never seem to affect you. Your smile is contagious. You appear to feast on the goodness of life and we get nourished by the crumbs that fall from your table. We love you for that. So, thank you!"

Suzy, a part-time teller, went next. "Patty, most of my friends are on the fast track to more money and climbing the corporate ladder in their careers. I have noticed you are one of those rare people who believe caring for others is somehow more important than notoriety, recognition, or promotion. That blows me away, and I want to honor you for that today."

Five more of the bank staff shared similar affirmations before it was George's turn. He glanced around at everyone and then turned to Patty. He reached in his coat pocket and pulled out the notes he had been working on at lunch. He looked at them, cleared his throat, and then did something unexpected. He folded the notes back up and returned them to his pocket. He thought, *No script for this*,

George. Just say what's in your heart. And with that thought, he began. . . .

"Patty, it's hard for me to put into words what your friendship, service to the bank, and life mean to me. There's a new word in my vocabulary that is helping me gain perspective on what's happened over the last month. It is the word *eu-catastrophic*. The word means— good-catastrophe. At first glance we all assume every catastrophe—whether an accident, a disaster, death, or tragedy—is terrible. And indeed, some are only that. They are full of pain, loss, and confusion. I think we would all agree your accident was terrible. It was a catastrophic event. But, I need to tell you today that the possibility of losing you in that accident has had a deep impact on me and in me. It was eu-catastrophic. Sitting in the ER with so many who love you created space for me to do some much-needed reflecting. It caused a clearing of the deck in my mind. It reminded me what's most important in life. It allowed me the opportunity to reevaluate how I should be living. To be truthful, before your accident, I felt a bit lost. We had a good long talk about this at the hospital as you recovered. You said some things I needed to hear. Thanks for speaking truth to me."

George paused and looked at the faces of his team members, "I'm guessing, from my lack of engagement at the bank this last year, most of you have sensed I've been out of sorts. The routine of everything, and the dreaded regulatory matters clouded my ability to see the road ahead. But now, for the first time in months, I am clear thinking and energized as I look at my future. For a while I forgot why I choose my vocation and why I do what I do. I got infected with the disease of me. That disease kills everything it touches—marriages, families, workplaces, and lives. Well, it's no longer about me. Moving forward, I'm recommitting to my core beliefs and values."

Turning back to Patty, George confessed, "Having to contemplate losing one of my dearest friends has been a gift to me because it reminded me of things I had forgotten. Thanks to the heart work I've been doing recently, I feel like a changed man. I recently made a friend who has taught me about a process of renewal and I have been following his suggestions—inspecting my life, redirecting accordingly, and taking action. I'm at the action step now, and each time I take action, it feels great. Bursts of energy fill me and I'm motivated to move ahead. I apologized to my wife, Anne, for being distant and insensitive. I called my sons and asked them to forgive me for not being understanding or supportive at points along the way. I also met with Morton Frazier to apologize for not being a better friend."

George turned his gaze from Patty. He slowly made eye contact with each person.

"I also want to apologize to all of you …"

Like when he made things right with Anne, George had to swallow hard to press down the emotions he was feeling. Patty reached out and put her hand on his arm. She smiled and offered a supportive nod.

"I am sorry for not being the leader you all deserve. I allowed us to lose sight of our core values. That's not going to happen again. I'm back, and I'm resolved for us to be the bank with a heart. The last thing I want to say to you, Patty, is thank you. Thanks for helping me recover my sense of life and purpose. We miss you and can't wait for your full return."

The staff exploded with applause. Everyone knew this was one of those special moments when you just couldn't help but cheer. They celebrated the fact that Patty was alive and going to have a full recovery, and they were glad their boss had found his way back and was facing the future renewed. And they whooped it up because the sweet taste of authentic community filled the place.

When things calmed Patty said, "All right, do I get a chance to speak now?"

George said, "What do you think everyone? Should we let Patty say a few words?"

In unison the chant of "Speech, speech, speech" broke out. Patty was beaming with pride and gratitude. Moments like these were what her life had always been about, and she was fully present breathing in the joy of friendship and appreciation. When the bank grew quiet, she began to share.

"Thank you everyone, thank you. You are such a special group of people. My heart has been filled by your generous comments. Getting knocked on your back for a while, I have discovered, isn't all bad. George, you've been doing some thinking about renewal over this last month, and I applaud you for that. Well, I've been doing some thinking about renewal too, and my thinking has led me to this conclusion: I'm not coming back to the bank."

There was a gasp as Patty's words sank in. The team was stunned. Suzy relayed what everyone was thinking when she said, "No, you can't leave!"

Maureen blurted out, "What do you mean you aren't coming back? We need you."

"You'll be fine without me, Maureen. You are more than capable to do my job." Grabbing George's arm, Patty said, "I'm recommending her, George."

George nodded as his eyes welled up with tears.

Patty continued, "Look everybody, there comes a moment when every person must muster the courage to chase her dream if she expects to stay fully engaged in life and renewed. And the application of courage is unique for each person. George, for you it took courage to stay at the bank and recover your purpose and passion. It required remembering who you are and why you do what you do. For me, courage looks different. Like you, George, I have spent time on introspection. I've thought long and hard and now it is time for redirection. For me the *action* requires a change. I don't want to look back on my life and have any regrets, or wish I had shown more courage. George, watching how courageous you have been has made me realize I want to be that brave. I've been thinking, *If you can do it, then I can do it.*"

Patty's affirmation of her now former boss caused everyone to laugh through their tears.

"There comes a moment when every person must muster the courage to chase their dream if they expect to stay renewed."

"Paul and I have thought and prayed together about how we should spend the next chapter of our lives. And as much as I love all of you and this place, I've decided I want to offer myself as a full-time volunteer to the women's shelter downtown. I have a real passion I can't shake for that cause, and I don't think I will be fulfilled unless I can give more time to it. I also have two amazing daughters and two grandsons who need more of me."

You could hear a pin drop as people sat looking at their role model, trying to get their minds around what the bank would be like post-Patty. It was George who broke the silence.

"Wow! Maybe I shouldn't have answered your call this morning. You didn't tell me it was going to be a retirement party. Patty, I must say, you never cease to surprise me. The thought of you not being here is scary. I guess we will all be required to show a bit of courage in the days ahead without our queen. But, I think this is a fantastic idea, and I'm 110 percent behind you. Who better than you to serve those women and help them rebuild their lives? Once you get a sense of how we can help, let us know. We are all behind you, and the bank will be the first in line to make a donation to the cause."

"Thank you, George. Thank you, everyone. You'll still see me. You can't get rid of me that easily. I still bank here, and the women's shelter banks here."

Looking at Maureen, Patty concluded with a sly grin, "Since I'm going to be a volunteer and you'll have a fancy new job, you will have to pay when we have lunch together."

Six Months Later

The Christmas Eve snow fell gently on the sidewalk of the bank as George locked the door and said goodbye to his assistant, Maureen. No longer just a teller on Tuesdays and Thursdays, in her new full-time role Maureen was proving to make a difference like her mentor, Patty.

It was noon, and George was about to start his end-of-year vacation. On the drive home he reflected on the past twelve months. It had started a year ago when his son, Mark, met a barista named Jim Clarke. He reflected with gratefulness on how Jim had not only helped Mark, but had also helped him gain perspective on his own life. Introspection, redirection, and action had truly led to traction. He reminisced on his relationship with Anne and how thankful he was to have such a great wife who had stood beside him when he had lost his way. And he thought of his hero, Patty Porter, who was in an accident that affected so many lives because someone had failed to pay attention to a STOP sign.

As George turned the corner into his neighborhood, he anticipated what was about to happen. In a moment he would walk in the door where he would find Anne preparing the table for a Christmas Eve party catered by Sarah Porter's new business. Mark would be arriving soon with his new girlfriend, Katie Clarke, and her parents, Jim and Sarah. And Patty and Paul would show up with some kind of gift.

The car came to a complete stop at George's favorite intersection. As he looked to his left he saw Officer Bradley sitting next to the curb a couple of driveways down. Bradley looked over in George's direction, and George nodded and smiled.

He had learned his lesson, and he felt renewed.

UNSTUCK

Application Guide

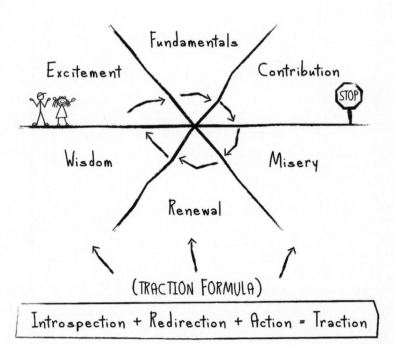

Applying the **Traction Formula**
and the **Six-Phase Model** to Your Life

You, the Traction Formula, and the Six-Phase Model

In our work with people from all walks of life, two critical truths have become clear to us. *First*, people tend to minimize the value of healthy self-leadership practices until they reach a point of fatigue or frustration. At this point, they realize that how they have done their life in the past won't get them to the life they desire. *Second*, it usually takes a discomforting STOP sign (some type of internal or external breakdown) to awaken them to the fact that how they are doing their life needs to change.

Almost every maturing person we know reaches a moment when he or she needs to get UNSTUCK by rethinking, or rediscovering—who they are at their core—what is it that will enable them to sustain making their contribution over the long run—and, how to integrate daily practices of renewal that keep them excited about life and work. If they have lost themselves in their work over the years, there may be a desire to rediscover who they are and why they do what they do. If they have been in a job contrary to how they are wired up, that incongruence needs to be corrected, even if it means a career change. If their job has changed significantly over time, but they have not, adjustments will need to be made.

Our desire for this Application Guide is to help you:

1. Identify and develop yourself wherever you are in the Six-Phase Model

2. Understand how to apply the Traction Formula to your current life circumstances
3. Guide you to establish regenerative practices that will enable you to make a sustained contribution to the world around you and experience lasting fulfillment in life.

This Field Guide is not meant to be exhaustive, but it will help you take the next step in creating a life of ongoing renewal. We hope you will consider attending one of the UNSTUCK Retreats we host around the county. Or maybe you will contact the authors and pursue a Personal Leadership Summit. These experiences can help you take additional steps in living renewed each day. For now, let's learn how to apply the Traction Formula to your life ... TODAY!

THE TRACTION FORMULA

$$\boxed{\text{Introspection} + \text{Redirection} + \text{Action} = \text{Traction}}$$

INTROSPECTION: *The examination or observation of one's own mental and emotional processes*

Deliberately inspecting your life has power. *Introspection* examines what's going on in and around you. You allow curiosity to become your friend. You step back and work through your sacred questions. You pay attention to how you feel and what you think about things. In essence, you develop the life skill of listening to your life. It is here that you get clear concerning the person you want to be *and* the life you want to live. Introspection will tell you where your life needs to change.

REDIRECTION: *The action of assigning or directing something to a new or different place or purpose*

As you recognize adjustments that need to be made it will call for areas of your life to be *redirected*. Imagine driving a car and you realize you are heading in the wrong direction. You are driving east and you should be heading west. It is not enough to recognize you are going in the wrong direction. It is not enough to just slow down. And it is not enough to stop the car. You must turn the car around and point it in a different direction. That's the shift that redirection calls for. It is unleashing your will on an area of life and creating a new compass setting.

ACTION: *The fact or process of actually doing something*

Now that you've pointed the car in the right direction, you must put your foot on the gas pedal and move. That's what *action* is about. You have come to the realization that things aren't right—you've decided on a new direction— now you take specific actions that will get you there.

TRACTION: *The action of pulling something forward*

Patiently working the Traction Formula will result in the needed *traction* to move you down the road toward life, joy, and renewal.

APPLYING THE TRACTION FORMULA TO THE SIX-PHASE MODEL

George Johnson is right in the middle of the *misery phase* when he sits down for coffee with Jim Clarke. As you look at the illustration of the Six-Phase Model below, think about what phase you are in. In this Application Guide we want to sit down for coffee with you and help you identify where you are and then understand how to apply the Traction Formula.

We will walk you through each phase and inform you of its purpose. We will then clarify in greater detail some of the core lessons to learn while there. Think carefully about what the Traction Formula means in each phase. The life skill of INTROSPECTING—REDIRECTING—and taking ACTION is something you will want to apply every day of your life, no matter which phase you are in.

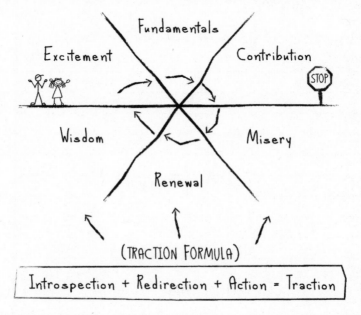

(TRACTION FORMULA)

Introspection + Redirection + Action = Traction

APPLYING THE TRACTION FORMULA TO THE SIX-PHASE MODEL

BEGINNINGS

To get started—identify which character in the fable that begins this book you most identify with at this time in your life.

- ☐ George Johnson
- ☐ Anne Johnson
- ☐ Jim Clarke
- ☐ Patty Porter
- ☐ Paul Porter
- ☐ Faith Porter
- ☐ Sarah Porter
- ☐ Morton Frazier
- ☐ Maureen

What is it about this person you most relate to?

_____

_____

_____

_____

_____

_____

_____

_____

_____

_____

As you look at the Traction Formula, which part do you understand the *least*?

INTROSPECTION + REDIRECTION + ACTION = TRACTION

- ☐ Introspection
- ☐ Redirection
- ☐ Action
- ☐ Traction

As you look at the Six-Phase Model, which phase do you think you are in?

- ☐ Excitement Phase
- ☐ Fundamentals Phase
- ☐ Contribution Phase
- ☐ Misery Phase
- ☐ Renewal Phase
- ☐ Wisdom Phase

What are the best and worst parts of this phase?

Best _____

_____

_____

_____

Worst _____

_____

_____

_____

Now, let's take a deeper look at each phase and see what we can learn.

EXCITEMENT PHASE

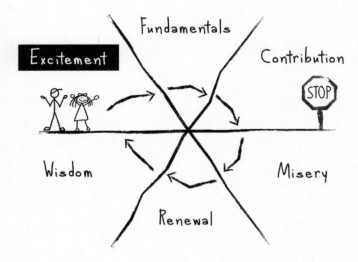

At the front end of most life experiences there is excitement. That could be a new job, relationship, birth of a child, or even attending college. Newness holds energy most of the time and that's the spark this first phase ignites. As you begin something new, it will need all the energy and positivity you can bring. In our twenties most of us have the energy of two people. Use this—leverage it.

PURPOSE of this phase: Energy to launch and engage the new

LESSONS of this phase: Clarifying identity and calling
Your *identity* is about who you are.
Your *calling* is about why you do what you do.

Suggestions for Growing in the Excitement Phase ...

Use your energy to your advantage. Being young and beginning a career is a beautiful thing. Use it to your advantage. Go in early and stay late.

At work, volunteer for additional projects that will expose you to other leaders and expand both your knowledge and experience. You will never be at a time where you can learn as fast or as much as right now. Step up when opportunities surface.

Respect those who are older and have more experience but less energy. Remember those who are older have experience that you don't. Their life and leadership stories can contribute to your growth, so honor, respect, and listen to them.

Take the time to think through both your identity and your calling. If you are in a job that is wrong for you, your inner world will talk back to you. You will sense something is off. That's why it's important to answer thoughtfully the questions on the following pages. It's important to validate you are in your sweet spot.

APPLYING THE EXCITEMENT PHASE...

IDENTITY QUESTIONS: *WHO YOU ARE DEEP DOWN*

What talents do I have that define my contribution?

What do I value most?

What are my most important core beliefs?

Applying the Excitement Phase ...(Cont)

Calling Questions: *Why You Chose Your Career*

What are my passions?

What do I think about when I'm in a good place?
Where does my mind drift?

Which of my childhood experiences have contributed to what I most value?

Applying the Traction Formula

Introspection + Redirection + Action = Traction

As you unleash your energy and excitement in your life and career, pay attention to healthy boundaries. It's hard to believe at this time of your life, but you aren't a super-hero. Be cautious about burning the candle at both ends for too long for too many days in a row. Just because you are young, you aren't immune to exhaustion and illness. Listen to your life and redirect yourself to healthier behaviors as needed. Take actions to rest on weekends and eat well. Habits you form in your twenties will carry into your thirties. If you are in the excitement phase, take a few minutes and apply the Traction Formula to a needed area of your life on the next two pages.

APPLYING THE TRACTION FORMULA IN THE EXCITEMENT PHASE

Rule Yourself and Write Your Story

INTROSPECTION
Where am I right now?

_____

_____

_____

_____

_____

_____

_____

_____

REDIRECTION
Where do I want to be?

_____

_____

_____

_____

_____

_____

_____

_____

```
                  ┌─────────────────────────┐
              ┌───┤          ACTION          ├───┐
              ╲   │  What steps will I take?  │   ╱
               ╲  └─────────────────────────┘  ╱
                ╲                             ╱
                 ╲_____╱
                 ╲                           ╱
                  ╲                         ╱
                   ╲                       ╱
                    ╲                     ╱
                     ╲_____╱
```

_____

_____

_____

_____

_____

_____

_____

_____

_____

_____

_____

_____

_____

_____

_____

_____

_____

_____

_____

_____

_____

_____

_____

_____

_____

FUNDAMENTALS PHASE

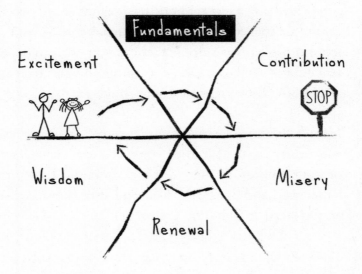

In every life role, whether that's parenting or being a surgeon, there are a set of fundamentals (or basics) you must grasp if you are to move ahead in life. How quickly these get identified, learned, and mastered has a lot to say about how fast you become effective and successful. Humility creates space inside you to learn from others. Be humble enough to stay *teachable*.

> PURPOSE of this phase: To prepare you to make your contribution
>
> LESSONS of this phase: Stay teachable, find a mentor, and recognize your current role is the most important one you will ever have.

SUGGESTIONS FOR GROWING IN THE FUNDAMENTALS PHASE ...

Study high performers. There are reasons some people do better than others. Keep a journal with learnings from those who are already where you want to be. Be teachable every day. Do everything you can to learn about how they grew to where they are.

Identify the fundamentals critical to success in your position and master them. Whether you are a cardiac surgeon or you plow snow, there are fundamentals that must be learned and mastered. Make a list of them and set action steps to help you grow.

Don't be afraid of failure. Ask for opportunities to stretch your skills and try new things. We grow as we try and fail—then we try and improve—then we try and succeed. If you aren't failing, you aren't growing.

Value the importance of being faithful in the little things. Your ability to be trusted will increase as you prove yourself capable in small things. Wisdom tells us that a person who is faithful in little will be faithful in much. So, be faithful in your current responsibilities. Do more than is expected and good things will happen.

APPLYING THE FUNDAMENTALS PHASE...

STUDY HIGH PERFORMERS

Who has your role in life and does it better than you?
List two people:

_____   _____

How will you connect to them and learn?

IDENTIFY THE CRITICAL FUNDAMENTALS AND MASTER THEM

List the five core fundamentals critical to success in your role. How will you grow in each?

Fundamental	Steps I'll Take to Grow
1. _____	_____
	_____
	_____
	_____
2. _____	_____
	_____
	_____
	_____
3. _____	_____
	_____
	_____
	_____
4. _____	_____
	_____
	_____
5. _____	_____
	_____
	_____

Don't Be Afraid of Failure

List two challenges you can take in your role where there is a risk of failure.

1. _____
   _____
2. _____
   _____

What could be the upside of not succeeding the first time you try?

Value the Importance of Being Faithful in the Little Things

What is one task/project/assignment you currently have that, if you do it really well, will demonstrate you can handle more responsibility?

Applying the Traction Formula

Introspection + Redirection + Action = Traction

It's somewhat easy to see how the Traction Formula can serve you during the Fundamentals Phase. There is a lot of learning going on during this phase. Being continually aware of what you don't know can be discouraging. This awareness comes through *introspection*. It's introspection that will point the way to how you need to grow. Focusing in on places of growth reveals where your skills need *redirecting*. Then you determine which *actions* to take that will create vocational traction. Discuss these with your boss and close friends … then pursue them. If you are in the Fundamentals Phase, take a few minutes and apply the Traction Formula to a needed area of your life on the next two pages.

APPLYING THE TRACTION FORMULA IN THE FUNDAMENTALS PHASE

Rule Yourself and Write Your Story

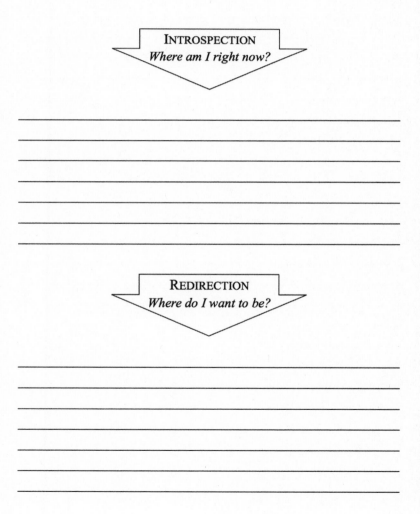

INTROSPECTION
Where am I right now?

_____

_____

_____

_____

_____

_____

_____

REDIRECTION
Where do I want to be?

_____

_____

_____

_____

_____

_____

_____

ACTION
What steps will I take?

_____
_____
_____
_____
_____
_____
_____
_____
_____
_____
_____
_____
_____
_____
_____
_____
_____
_____
_____
_____
_____
_____
_____
_____
_____
_____
_____

CONTRIBUTION PHASE

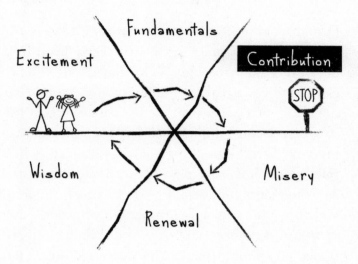

As a maturing person you have a responsibility to bring the full weight of your talent and energy to your job and life. You have learned much along the way and are mastering the fundamentals. You are willing and able to carry more and more responsibility. The critical core lessons have been learned and competency has been reached—now it's time to show up daily and do what you do.

PURPOSE of this phase: Make a meaningful contribution

LESSONS of this phase: Keep your passions hot for what you do, mentor those younger than you, and begin to look for life mentors

Suggestions for Growing in the Contribution Phase

Own what it means to keep your passion hot for what you do. Being in this phase means you have been fulfilling your role for a while. The routine of your role can rough you up over time. It can affect your excitement for what you are doing. Because of this, it's easy to lose a sense of importance for how you are investing your life. This means your passion can fade. *It's your responsibility to keep your heart engaged in what you do.* Some ideas for keeping your passion hot: identify and surround yourself with people who remind you of the importance of what you do, figure out what books you should read to inspire you—and attend conferences (or listen to podcasts) that rekindle your sense of importance for how you are investing your life.

Mentor the next generation. In the previous phase you were challenged to find a mentor. Now, it's your turn to help someone behind you grow. All along the way you have been learning and increasing your competence. Every lesson you have learned is fodder for the mentoring of those after you. Identify a couple of emerging leaders, take them to lunch, and add value to their lives. When you do this it will both validate your growth and encourage you to keep growing.

Begin to look for a life mentor. As you age there will be an increased desire to interact with those who are further up the road. These people are wiser and more experienced. You can talk with them about work, but more important, you can talk with them about life.

APPLYING THE CONTRIBUTION PHASE...

KEEP YOUR PASSIONS HIGH

Has your role changed recently? If so, how?

List the names of three people who fire you up about the importance of your work. How, and when, will you next connect with them? *(phone call, coffee, lunch, activity?)*

WHO?_____

WHEN?_____

HOW?_____

WHO?_____

WHEN?_____

HOW?_____

WHO?_____

WHEN?_____

HOW?_____

List a book you will read this month that will inspire you in your work.

What conference can you attend (or podcast can you listen to) to energize you?

MENTOR THOSE YOUNGER THAN YOU

List the names of two younger people you can mentor. When and how will you connect with them?

WHO?_____

WHEN?_____

HOW?_____

WHO?_____

WHEN?_____

HOW?_____

What have you learned that those younger need to know?
(Remember … it's about adding value to them.)

Identify a Life Mentor

List the names of two possible life mentors. Who are they?

_____

_____

Given where you are today, what are two questions (or issues) you would like to discuss with them?

_____

_____

_____

_____

_____

_____

Applying the Traction Formula during the Contribution Phase

Introspection + Redirection + Action = Traction

Paying attention to your passion level is the work of introspection. If your passion has faded for life and work, redirect yourself to passion-producing input. Whether it's people, books, or conferences, you must take action to stoke the fire in you for what you do. You will have to think about who you want to mentor and take a step toward them. Pay attention to what you feel as you run names through your mind. If you take a step toward someone and it doesn't work, redirect and try someone else. The same is true in pursuing a life mentor. We hope that by the time you get to this phase in life you are daily reflecting, making necessary changes, and taking the right next steps. If you are in the contribution phase, take a few minutes and apply the Traction Formula to a needed area of your life on the next two pages.

APPLYING THE TRACTION FORMULA IN THE CONTRIBUTION PHASE

Rule Yourself and Write Your Story

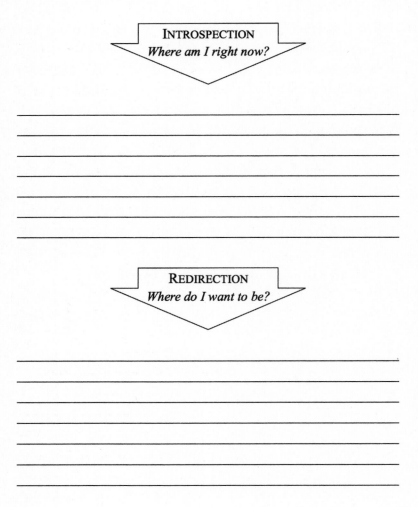

INTROSPECTION
Where am I right now?

_____

_____

_____

_____

_____

_____

_____

REDIRECTION
Where do I want to be?

_____

_____

_____

_____

_____

_____

_____

ACTION
What steps will I take?

_____
_____
_____
_____
_____
_____
_____
_____
_____
_____
_____
_____
_____
_____
_____
_____
_____
_____
_____
_____
_____
_____
_____
_____
_____
_____

STOP Sign

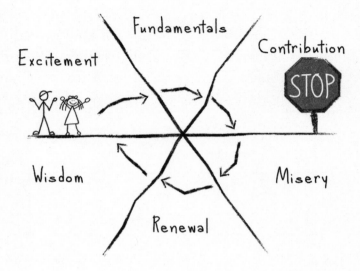

STOP signs exist for a purpose. Ignoring a STOP sign can result in trouble. Wisdom pays attention. There are many ways to deal with an unwanted STOP sign. Here are a few: ignore it, deny that it's there, or pretend nothing is wrong. Others will try to irrigate the discomfort by pleasuring the pain away. Some manage it by running back to the *excitement phase* and taking a new job or engaging a new project. None of those options move a person toward renewal. The best option for those who long for renewal is to walk into, and through, the *misery phase*.

PURPOSE of the STOP sign: To get your attention
LESSONS of the STOP sign: See the pain as a friend, and avoid harmful pain management strategies

Suggestions for Growing at a STOP Sign

Avoid the house of pleasure. Solomon, described in ancient literature as the wisest man who ever lived, said in Ecclesiastes 7:4, "*The mind of the wise is in the house of mourning, while the mind of the fool is in the house of pleasure.*" He says really smart people—*the wise*—embrace discomfort and learn from the pain of life. They will know times of sadness—*mourning*—when they sit at the feet of their own pain and learn. Others—*fools*—handle it differently. Their strategy is to run down the well-worn path to the house of pleasure. The house of pleasure is an illusion. It offers temporary relief but no long-term solution to the real problem one is facing. People become addicted to all sorts of stuff in the house of pleasure—drugs, alcohol, sex, binge watching, thrills, you name it. It's a dead-end strategy to deal with the inner pain one is feeling. Solomon knew what he was talking about.

Identify a trusted friend and share where you are. Finding someone older and wiser is critical when you hit a STOP sign. Who might that be for you? A parent, grandparent, pastor, counselor, friend, or trusted coworker? Given all you are feeling at this time, lonely is not one you want to add.

Remember that you aren't the first person to hit a STOP sign. It's tempting to think nobody could possibly understand what you are going through. Both authors thought that when they hit their STOP signs. Trust that there are people around you who care.

Applying the STOP Sign...

Let the STOP Sign Get Your Attention

When did you first sense you were at a STOP sign?
What caused you to think this?

Avoid the House of Pleasure

Up to this point, what has been your strategy to deal
with your STOP sign and the accompanying pain?

Applying the Traction Formula at the STOP Sign

Introspection + Redirection + Action = Traction

If you are sensing you are at a STOP sign, *introspection* is in play. Be honest with yourself and reflect on where you are and how you are feeling. Be curious about it instead of cursing it. If you have been using poor methods to deal with your pain, redirect yourself into the house of mourning and listen. The needed action is to rally the courage to step into, and through, the *misery phase*. Trust that good things can come from this time. Use the next two pages to identify your next step.

APPLYING THE TRACTION FORMULA AT THE STOP SIGN

Rule Yourself and Write Your Story

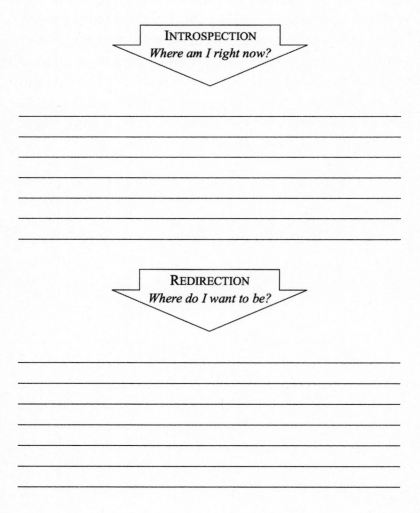

INTROSPECTION
Where am I right now?

_____
_____
_____
_____
_____
_____

REDIRECTION
Where do I want to be?

_____
_____
_____
_____
_____
_____

ACTION
What steps will I take?

_____
_____
_____
_____
_____
_____
_____
_____
_____
_____
_____
_____
_____
_____
_____
_____
_____
_____
_____
_____
_____
_____
_____
_____
_____
_____

MISERY PHASE

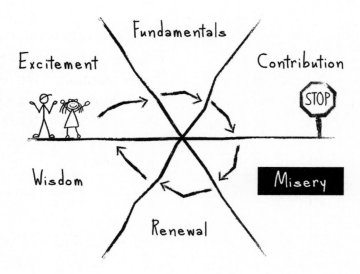

Misery shows its ugly face in many ways. You can feel bored with life. You might sense fatigue on a soul level. Or, you could be disillusioned with how things are going in your life. Misery can shut you down or open you up to consider some really important questions. Identifying the *sacred questions* is critical to moving ahead toward renewal. Rallying the courage to be painfully honest and putting your truth on the table is difficult, scary, and desperately needed at this point.

PURPOSE of this phase: Identity your sacred questions
LESSON of this phase: Without honesty you are going nowhere

Suggestions for Growing in the Misery Phase...

Identify your sacred questions. A sacred question is one, which if answered, can help you understand how to find your way to renewal. These questions have the power to peel back life and allow you to see the contributing factors to your current situation. Sacred questions push us deeper into ourselves so we can get to the root of what's blocking joy and life.

Don't skirt the brutal truth of things. Some of your sacred questions will be difficult to answer. You have to figure out what has contributed to how you currently feel. What has changed recently? What's caused that change? How have the changes affected you? Sometimes there have been changes at work that had real consequence to you. At other times these changes have no effect at all. You need to sort this all out. Have the courage to put the truth on the table and be brutally honest as you look at your life.

Understand you are entering a process. Everything gets done in process. It will take time to hike up the mountain, then turn around, and look at the valley floor of your life to gain perspective. Be patient.

APPLYING THE MISERY PHASE...

IDENTIFY SACRED QUESTIONS

What has changed both in and around me over the past few years?

How can my talent touch the world and bring me deep joy?

What kind of person/spouse/parent/friend do I want to be?

When it's all said and done, what legacy do I want to leave?

What other sacred questions need to be considered and answered?

- _____
  _____

- _____
  _____

- _____
  _____

- _____
  _____

- _____
  _____

- _____
  _____

- _____
  _____

- _____
  _____

Applying the Traction Formula during the Misery Phase

Introspection + Redirection + Action = Traction

Healthy introspection is critical at this point. Rallying the energy and courage to turn from anger, frustration, and disillusionment will be critical. Bravery will be required as you redirect yourself from unhealthy feelings to working the process that will get you to renewal. Just take one step at a time. Use the next two pages to identify where you are and the next steps you will take.

APPLYING THE TRACTION FORMULA IN THE MISERY PHASE

Rule Yourself and Write Your Story

INTROSPECTION
Where am I right now?

_____

_____

_____

_____

_____

_____

_____

REDIRECTION
Where do I want to be?

_____

_____

_____

_____

_____

_____

_____

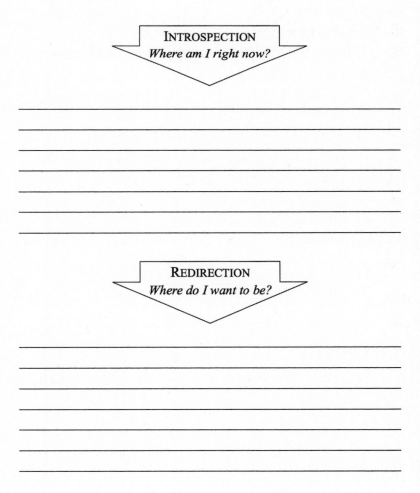

ACTION
What steps will I take?

_____
_____
_____
_____
_____
_____
_____
_____
_____
_____
_____
_____
_____
_____
_____
_____
_____
_____
_____
_____
_____
_____
_____
_____
_____
_____

RENEWAL PHASE

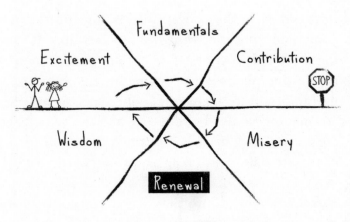

(TRACTION FORMULA)
Introspection + Redirection + Action = Traction

Although the traction formula should be in play in every part of the Six-Phase Model, this is where it gets fully engaged. It's here you take a deep breath, look at who you are, and get clear on how you got to this place of discontent. Change happens here if you have the courage to look at your life, decide your future, and move in that direction. The renewal you long for will come as a by-product of the work you do in this phase. The traction formula charts the pathway to renewal.

> PURPOSE of this phase: Introspect, redirect, and take action
>
> LESSONS of this phase: Own your life, do your work, and anticipate the graces to come

Traction Formula

Introspection + Redirection + Action = Traction

Introspection is the process of blazing the trail into your inner world of thought and emotion. It's paying attention to yourself. We don't want to become lost in the inner world of thought and emotion, but it's important to be curious about why you are where you are. It is vital to be reflective and analyze why you feel as you do. This develops the *listen to your life* skill needed to gain traction and move forward.

Redirection comes into play when you look at your story and decide you want to head a different direction. It is the mental and willful decision of choosing to write your new story. At the places in your life where you are heading in the wrong direction, redirection steps up and chooses the path *you* desire.

Action is the activation part of redirection. Nothing changes until you take action. Actually doing something is demanded. Take one step at a time.

Suggestions for Growing in the Renewal Phase...

Own your life. This seems obvious, but it's not. Many people either wait for someone to save them or cope by blaming others for their life circumstances. The truth is, you must *rule yourself.* You cannot expect anyone to step in and save you here. It's your life and you must step forward and do the work of renewal. Choosing to do your work because others will benefit is a good motivation. There is nothing wrong with pursuing health and wholeness because you love your family and coworkers. But here, you chose to move ahead because you love yourself enough to do the work.

Do your work. You know what it means to work. You are where you are in life because of the hard work you have done. Things weren't given to you, you went after them. It will take at least the same effort to do your renewal work, gain traction, and move forward. You haven't shied away from tough tasks in the past, and you won't here either. So, put on your workout clothes and step toward renewal.

Anticipate the graces to come. Here's the good news: there are graces, meaningful gifts, to be received along the way as you take the right steps forward. Goodness comes to those who don't back up. Some of those graces will be the new friends you will make, the healing of childhood issues, the mentoring you get from the books you read, and the fresh definition of the future life you will pursue. These are just a few of the graces to come. Overall, you will love what it feels like on the other side of this process.

APPLYING THE TRACTION FORMULA...

Introspection + Redirection + Action = Traction

INTROSPECTION

Go back to the *misery phase* and look at your list of sacred questions (pages 180-181). Be curious about your answers. What insights did you gain from answering those four questions?

REDIRECTION

Where specifically in your life are you heading in an unhealthy direction?

Action

What steps will you take that will move you in the right direction?

Traction

As you work this process, where are you sensing traction?

APPLYING THE RENEWAL PHASE...

ANTICIPATE THE GRACES TO COME

What graces have come your way as you have been working the Traction Formula in this phase? (Met any great people? Read any insightful books? Identified any lies you've been believing? Have any fresh insights concerning the truth about you? Had any breakthroughs in your understanding of life? Any others?)

List them:

- _____
  _____
- _____
  _____
- _____
  _____
- _____
  _____
- _____
  _____
- _____
  _____
- _____
  _____
- _____
  _____

Use the next two pages to clarify your next steps.

APPLYING THE TRACTION FORMULA IN THE RENEWAL PHASE

Rule Yourself and Write Your Story

INTROSPECTION
Where am I right now?

_____
_____
_____
_____
_____
_____
_____

REDIRECTION
Where do I want to be?

_____
_____
_____
_____
_____
_____
_____

ACTION
What steps will I take?

_____

_____

_____

_____

_____

_____

_____

_____

_____

_____

_____

_____

_____

_____

_____

_____

_____

_____

_____

_____

_____

_____

_____

_____

_____

WISDOM PHASE

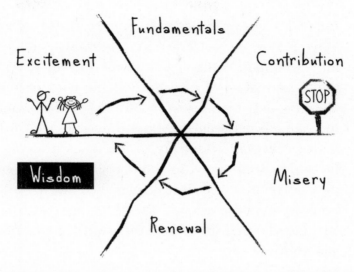

Wisdom collects life lessons along the way. Sometimes we learn best when life is hard or we fail. Wisdom is applying your life experience to future behavior. There is no shame in failing unless you fail again for the same reason. There is no disgrace in going through a difficult experience unless you fail to grow. This phase allows you time to identify and record the lessons you have learned along the way through the process.

> PURPOSE of this phase: Identify and record lessons learned along the way and declare the life you want to live from here on out
>
> LESSONS of this phase: Establish regenerative practices, learn to live in the tensions mature people understand, and recognize the difference between the first and second halves of life

Suggestions for Growing in the Wisdom Phase...

Establish regenerative practices that renew and refresh. What renews and refreshes you? Seriously, is it reading? Solitude? Walking in nature? Music? Prayer? Golf? Journaling? Recreation? Being with friends? Working out? Painting? You have to find the balance in your life between the expending and replenishing of energy. The activity of life tends to deplete. Declaring what activities pour back into you, and putting them on your calendar, is critical. What renews you in the second half of life might be different than the first half. Make this personal, practical, and positive.

Be mindful of the tensions mature people learn to live in. Mature people understand and live in the tension between—self and others—work and rest—giving and receiving—energy out and energy in. We don't live in Utopia, so we have to navigate reality. Identifying and understanding these tensions impart grace to manage life.

Recognize the difference between the first and second halves of life. The first half of life is more about energy, climbing, and getting good at our work. The second half is more about depth, congruence, authentic self, and character. It could be said we move from the work we do in the first half to a deeper look at our lives in the second half.

APPLYING THE WISDOM PHASE...

ESTABLISH REGENERATIVE PRACTICES THAT RENEW AND REFRESH

Make a list of activities that refuel and refresh you.

- _____

- _____

- _____

- _____

- _____

Which of these need to be experienced daily? Weekly? Monthly? Yearly?

- Daily: _____

- Weekly: _____

- Monthly: _____

- Yearly: _____

Of these activities, which will you do this week? When will you do it?

Be Mindful of the Tensions Mature People Are Able to Balance

Below (and at the top of the next page) are a number of tensions mature people learn to live with. You will have a bias toward one side of this tension or the other. Circle the one that comes most naturally to you and then record on the line below one action you can take to compensate for your bias and live with greater balance. Remember, mature people understand that balance is learning to live in the center of the tension.

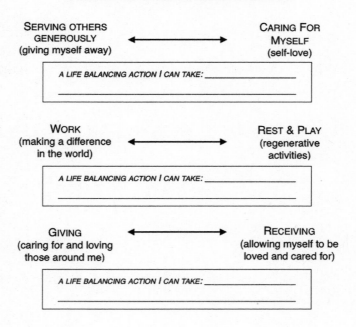

TENSIONS WE MUST LEARN TO LIVE WITH

SERVING OTHERS
GENEROUSLY
(giving myself away)
⟷
CARING FOR
MYSELF
(self-love)

A LIFE BALANCING ACTION I CAN TAKE: _____
_____

WORK
(making a difference
in the world)
⟷
REST & PLAY
(regenerative
activities)

A LIFE BALANCING ACTION I CAN TAKE: _____
_____

GIVING
(caring for and loving
those around me)
⟷
RECEIVING
(allowing myself to be
loved and cared for)

A LIFE BALANCING ACTION I CAN TAKE: _____
_____

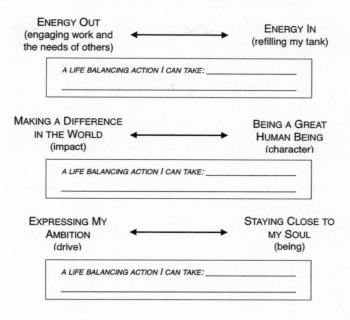

ENERGY OUT
(engaging work and
the needs of others)

ENERGY IN
(refilling my tank)

A LIFE BALANCING ACTION I CAN TAKE: _____
_____

**MAKING A DIFFERENCE
IN THE WORLD**
(impact)

**BEING A GREAT
HUMAN BEING**
(character)

A LIFE BALANCING ACTION I CAN TAKE: _____
_____

**EXPRESSING MY
AMBITION**
(drive)

**STAYING CLOSE TO
MY SOUL**
(being)

A LIFE BALANCING ACTION I CAN TAKE: _____
_____

Whom do you know who appears to live with grace and maturity in these tensions? *(two names)*

_____   _____

When will you connect with them?

What other wisdom lessons have you learned?

- _____

_____

- _____

_____

- _____

_____

- _____

_____

- _____

_____

- _____

_____

APPLYING THE WISDOM PHASE...

As you reflect on how you've applied the traction formula, what are the two best lessons you have learned that have made you wiser?

- _____
  _____
  _____
  _____
  _____
  _____

- _____
  _____
  _____
  _____
  _____
  _____

CREATING A PERSONAL MANIFESTO

How Do You Want Your Story to Play Out?

At the end of The Fable, Jim Clarke encourages George Johnson to create a document he can continually revisit and update. Some people call this document a "Personal Manifesto." It doesn't matter what you call it, just be sure to create it. This document will be the ongoing fruit of your work during the renewal phase and should articulate the person you want to be and the life you want to live. This tells the story of how your extraordinary life will play out moving forward. It's the new story—the best story of you. On the following pages you can begin this document. Every time the busyness of life chokes you and you feel like you have lost your way, come back and reread (and rewrite if necessary) this declaration. It will *redirect* you toward the life you want. Tweak it as needed. This document will declare your life purpose. Living out your purpose in an *action*-oriented way is critical for ongoing renewal. Read this every week for the next six months. This is one of the regenerative practices to do in the days ahead. You may only write a couple of sentences in each section following. That's okay, begin there.

PERSONAL MANIFESTO

My life purpose is: *(I think my life is to be about ...)*

_____

_____

_____

_____

_____

_____

_____

_____

_____

_____

_____

_____

_____

_____

_____

_____

_____

_____

_____

_____

_____

_____

_____

_____

_____

_____

_____

Personal Manifesto

I want my character to be defined by:

_____
_____
_____
_____
_____
_____
_____

The way I treat my life partner will be marked by:

_____
_____
_____
_____
_____
_____
_____

As a parent I will:

_____
_____
_____
_____
_____
_____
_____

Personal Manifesto

I want my personal spiritual life to be defined by:

_____
_____
_____
_____
_____
_____

At work I want to be known for:

_____
_____
_____
_____
_____
_____

As a friend I will:

_____
_____
_____
_____
_____
_____

Personal Manifesto

In my community I will:

_____
_____
_____
_____
_____
_____
_____

This defines how I will treat my body:

_____
_____
_____
_____
_____
_____
_____

The legacy I want to leave:

_____
_____
_____
_____
_____
_____
_____

PERSONAL MANIFESTO

Additional Thoughts:

_____

_____

_____

_____

_____

_____

_____

_____

_____

_____

_____

_____

_____

_____

_____

_____

_____

_____

_____

_____

_____

_____

_____

_____

_____

_____

_____

_____

_____

_____

SUGGESTIONS FOR THOSE WHO LEAD OTHERS

AN IMPORTANT FOUNDATIONAL THOUGHT FOR LEADER DEVELOPMENT

Leader development is a 'both–and' proposition. There are two lifelong works of leader development that the metaphor of a sailboat beautifully illustrates. Understanding both works will be critical to you wisely overseeing the development of others under your care. Consider the simple drawing below.

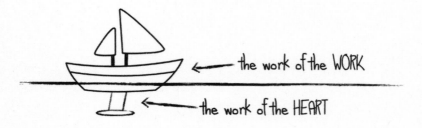

As you look at the sketch, notice there are two aspects to the sailboat as it sits on the water. The first is *above the waterline*, and the second is *beneath the waterline*. Above the waterline is visible and easily seen. We could compare it to the outward expression of our lives. Beneath the waterline is hidden, and we could say it represents the part of us that is not so easily seen: our heart, attitudes, character, integrity, and so on. As you look at the sailboat drawing, you can see the masts, two sails, and, if we could draw with greater detail, you'd see the deck, winches, railing, the wheel, and so on. The point is that above the water-line it's all seen, it's visible, and beneath it's not.

Above the waterline represents what we have come to call "the work of the work." This work informs us there is a work, a vocation if you will, with your name on it. How cool is that? Every person has been entrusted with gifts, talents, and passions. We are to follow those clues to, we hope, a work that energizes us and we are able to do. This work is personal. It should flow from our interests. It is found at the intersection of what we love and what we discover we are gifted to do. It allows our talent to touch the world in a productive and meaningful way. It is up to each person to do the work of discovering his or her passions and talents, and then developing them so they can accomplish *their* work.

Beneath the waterline is "the work of the HEART." This has to do with the type of human being we are each becoming. It is about the person we are, our wholeness, and some would say, our soul. It is who we are under the surface when no one is looking. Every day we choose what type of person we will become. There are a lot of very intelligent and talented people who have graduate degrees but who lack healthy core character. The vast majority of leadership breakdown begins beneath the waterline. The kind of person we become is the result of choices we make to live out of a healthy set of values and beliefs.

What we want you to understand with the sailboat sketch is this: For the rest of your life these two works will be in play every day. How you interact with each, during different seasons of life, reveals volumes concerning who you are and who you become. Whether a person is seventeen or seventy, he or she should be about trying to identify and accomplish the work with their name on it—the work of the work. He or she should also daily be about becoming the right kind of person—the work of the HEART. It is a *both–and* proposition—above *and* below—competence *and* character.

Suggestions for Leading People in the Different Phases

Many of the readers of this book lead teams of people in different arenas of life. You may be one of them. Leading a team of people to accomplish a meaningful goal can be both exhilarating and complicated. A needed critical leadership skill is to be able to discern where a person is and then help him or her develop. Both authors have led teams of people who were at different times in their careers. We have coached athletic teams, we are each dads to grown children, and we both have been responsible for building teams in our professional lives. We have each held positions that demanded the hiring, development, and sometimes firing of people. We understand that teams are made up of individuals who are at various stages of development. Next we offer a few suggestions for how to engage and challenge those you lead no matter what phase of life they are currently experiencing.

Leading People in the Excitement Phase

Never shame a young leader for their enthusiasm or optimism. You may be a little further up the road. You might be tainted by the "real world" of experience. Don't rob those in this phase of the joy of beginning. It is the responsibility of those in leadership to create space for young leaders. As you lead those in this phase, give them room to run. Leverage their energy.

Look for ways to challenge young leaders.
Young leaders usually have energy to burn. Give them challenging projects that will push them, reveal their abilities, and call out their best.

Encourage them to do the work of clarifying their identity and calling.
Best performance flows from those who love what they do and are good at it. Allow these young leaders to test themselves and learn what authentically fires them up. If they underperform, assess whether their talents can be applied differently.

Leading People in the Fundamentals Phase

Remember the 70/20/10 principle.
The latest thinking in leader development tells us people grow best if 70 percent of their time is spent in stretch activities, 20 percent interacting with mentors and peers, and 10 percent in classroom experiences.

The 70 percent is where the action is.
Identify meaningful stretch activities that will genuinely challenge those under your leadership. Do what you can to have them relate to others of different ages and experience levels. Put them on teams with different types of people that will stretch and grow them.

Make it real.
Identify real challenges, not busy work. If you'd be bored doing it, they probably will too. Make these stretch activities really stretching.

Facilitate honest feedback.

Be sure you debrief their performance, how they grew during the challenge, and what they can do to get better in the future. Find out what they learned and then tee up another challenge. Remind them regularly that it's not about perfection but effort and growth.

Celebrate their effort.

Too few bosses give out encouragement and affirmation. Don't be one of those bosses. Telling them how they did a good job will inspire high performance in the future.

Be vulnerable about your failures and experiences with growing.

Don't give off the vibe or pretend in front of them that you woke up one day and had everything together. Model honest sharing. Be transparent and vulnerable with them about times when you had to receive tough feedback and what you did to grow. It's your vulnerability that will open them to the things you have to teach. Tell them about times when you didn't learn quickly. Encourage them to keep growing.

Leading People in the Contribution Phase

Value their contribution.

This person has been part of your team for years fulfilling his or her role. Do they feel appreciated for the work they have done and are doing? Remind them of their value.

Occasionally create a safe space for them to talk honestly about their work.

It's not your job to keep them excited about the work they are paid to do, but it is wise to monitor their energy for the work they have been assigned. People tend to give their best effort for leaders who care about them. So, when you do your meeting with them occasionally ask them about how they are doing and their dreams for the future.

Help them identify ways to keep their passion high concerning the work they do.

Try to connect them with people who will fire them up and lift their performance. Suggest books that have been meaningful to you. Keep an eye out for growth opportunities or inspirational conferences you could send them to. Investing in people is the best thing you can do to improve the bottom line. An energized and challenged workforce brings its "A" game every day.

LEADING PEOPLE AT THE STOP SIGN

Be understanding; don't tell them to go fix themselves.

Helping someone at this place in life will be incredibly challenging because there is work they are responsible to accomplish. You also know that this person is a human being in need of support, understanding, and assistance. Balancing compassion *and* performance expectations will be dicey. So, what do you do?

Give them freedom to be honest with where they are. Ask them what they need from you. Offer whatever resources your organization has available. If an additional day off would help them create a strategy to seek perspective and healing, try to always come down on the side of grace. Suggest they seek the help of a counselor to walk them through this time. Finally, discuss the work they are responsible to do. Often just knowing you are in their corner will give them the added strength to keep doing their job as they face the difficulty of current life circumstances. One other thought, it probably is not a good idea to add any extra work to their current load as they navigate the *misery phase*.

LEADING PEOPLE IN THE MISERY PHASE

Be wise concerning the tension you face being both leader and friend.

Helping someone at this place in life will be challenging for many reasons. The first is that you must live in the tension between the work that must be done and the well-being of this person. You daily live aware of the work that must be accomplished, that's a given. You are also concerned for the well-being of this person on your team. How much room you give this person to figure things out depends partly on the quality of team player they have been and the past work they have done. If they have been with you ten years as a high performer, they should receive more grace than someone who has been with you six months and is a low performer. When in doubt, show grace and mercy.

Empathy is a must.

Listening is the key to empathy. Take time to really listen to what's going on in this person's life. It's not your job to fix his or her life, but it is your job to be human and understanding. Veteran leaders learn to do this with grace. A person at this place is often bored, tired, and disillusioned. If you care for him or her you will long for them to make their full contribution at work (that's a given), *but* we hope you will also desire for them to live a wholehearted and happy life. Helping this person create a plan that will move them to a place of health and full contribution is the goal. See if you can connect them with more senior people in your organization who have weathered such a time. Recognize that your personal management meetings will need to be safe for them to be honest concerning where they are. Surprise them with understanding as they work to find renewal. If you treat this person humanly it will motivate them to bring their best to their job once they regain traction.

Leading People at the Renewal Phase

Remember that leadership development is not all about skills, it's also about character and heart—so, offer encouragement, not shame.

We hope the person you are leading has (and is) working hard to increase their capability and capacity. Continually encourage them in that direction through training and accountability. Be mindful that he or she is in a season when their leadership has the potential to grow in a different area. In the story of George Johnson we mention that the first half of life tends to be mostly about the work of the work. During that time one identifies the work with one's name on it and does everything they can to keep improving. It's mainly about growing leadership skills and competency. This is leadership *above the waterline*. The person you are leading is currently entering a time of engaging the work of the heart. This is *beneath the waterline* and has to do with character, depth, healing, and wisdom. When he or she comes out on the other side you will have a more mature and capable team member. Valuing this time of development is important. Making fun of someone at this place is cruel, shortsighted, and foolish. Don't ever go there.

Check in weekly to see how they are doing and offer creative assistance if they are stuck.
The inner world of thought and emotion can be confusing to understand and scary to investigate. Ultimately you want a clear thinking, full-hearted, totally engaged team member. Helping them remove the inner clutter so they can bring their best self to work each day will serve you and the organization. We also know from experience that you will engender trust and maximize performance when you treat a team member with respect and patience.

Celebrate breakthroughs—even if they are small.
In your update conversations with this person point out and celebrate growth whenever you see it. They may feel nothing is changing. If you see things are on an upward swing, point it out and celebrate it.

Leading People in the Wisdom Phase

Encourage them to identify the graces that have come through the process and celebrate each.

Take the time to identify and discuss all the good things that have emerged from the tough time. Where has there been growth? What fresh life lessons have been learned? What new people were met? What inspiring books were read? Giving this person time to identify and value this growth will elevate the value they bring to the team.

Have them read to you their Personal Manifesto.

A great gift you can give to the one you lead is to nudge them to create their personal manifesto. Consider doing this with the entire team. Having your entire team do this exercise will energize and unify the team members. It is not easy work, but it is worth the effort. Having everyone create a personal manifesto will focus each life and call each person to live courageously by design rather than by default. It will do the same for you as you share your own personal manifesto. When that happens you can become a cheerleader for them as they strive to live the life they've always wanted.

Acknowledgments

It's a heck of a thing to have people in your life who love and believe in you. That begins with my wife of more than forty years—Judy Ann—and our three grown sons—Luke, Landan (his beautiful wife, Tiffany), and Logan. Then there are people who care about what I do and make it possible for me to do it. People like Denny and Scoob Ellens, Jim and Lynn Eickhoff, Ruth and Alan Breuker, Brian and Mary Lubinski, Dave and Lori Chow, along with Gus and Jenny Gustafson. A big "thanks" also goes out to the many people who stepped up, read the book, and offered valuable insight and perspective. Thanks to Jeannie and Larry Koops (my medical and finance brainiacs), Terry Schulenberg (my go-to friend with great skill and deep relational insight), Jim Raymond (a man who personifies courage and always sees the other side of the leaf), Juan Ortiz (the guy lives his faith), Tony Schwartz (the student who has become the teacher), Jimmy Page (the most positive man on the planet), Jason Stockton (the dude just keeps growing), Kathy Jo Fredette (insightful and deeply devoted to helping kids grow), Linda Lindquist-Bishop (as bright and tough as they come), and Troy Murphy (an incredible creative solutionist). My hope and prayer is that all "our" work will help many find traction, renewal, and joy in their life and work.

— Dan Webster

There was a time when I lacked traction in my life and work. Thankfully, I had a team of people who helped me rediscover my passion. Without them, this book would have never been written. I'm grateful for my coauthor, Dan Webster, who has served as a coach and close friend for nearly two decades. Mark Miller is the best leader I know, and I am blessed to call him my mentor and friend. His wisdom strengthened this book. A special thanks to Jon Gordon who encouraged me throughout this project and connected me to the great team at Wiley. Susan Barber provided excellent insight and helped make the book better with her red pen. John Orr was the first to challenge me to go public with my writing in a small-town paper twenty years ago. He also invested time in reading the first draft of this book and gave valuable encouragement. Chuck Cusumano has been my encourager around this topic for more than a decade. A man could ask for no one better to be in his corner. Laura, you are my best friend and inspiration. I treasure you. And to my four daughters, Hannah, Sarah, Rebekah, and Katherine, you are my deepest joy. Thank you for challenging me to live with courage, I'm proud of you, and I pray you will continue to walk in Truth.

— Randy Gravitt

About the Authors

Dan Webster is a lifelong student, practitioner, and pioneer in the area of leadership and life development. He has worked with numerous senior leaders across multiple sectors in the for-profit, nonprofit, para-church, educational, and church worlds. Dan served on the staff of two influential churches where he had the opportunity to build two of the largest and most effective student  ministries in America. Dan has been a visiting professor at numerous graduate schools on both the master's and PhD level. Recently, he has been a distinguished visiting scholar in the Values-Driven Leadership PhD/DBA program at Benedictine University outside of Chicago, Illinois.

In 1995 he founded *Authentic Leadership, Inc.* Since then he has devoted his life to speaking, writing, and mentoring leaders young and old both inside and outside the church.

As a communicator and mentor, Dan has presented on numerous occasions at conferences and events in South America, Europe, Canada, and all across the United States. His audiences enjoy his honesty, authenticity, and sense of humor. His messages hit the head and the heart with practical steps that move the listener toward the life they are meant to live.

Dan and his wife Judy have been married for more than forty years and live in Holland, Michigan. They have three grown sons: Luke, Landan (and a beautiful daughter-in-law, Tiffany), and Logan.

You can connect with Dan at www.danwebster.com.

Randy Gravitt is an author, speaker, and life coach who spends his time encouraging leaders to reach their potential. He has worked in education, both as a teacher and coach, served for eighteen years on the staff of one of the largest churches in the Atlanta area, and taught high-performance  leadership to companies and teams all over the world. His audiences are drawn to his encouragement and motivational style of speaking aimed at bringing about transformation.

In 2014 Randy founded INTEGREAT Leadership (www.integreatleadership.com), a company whose mission is to grow a generation of integrity-driven leaders. His current work includes training high-performance leadership teams for Chick-fil-A, Inc., and serving as one of the leadership coaches for the Pittsburgh Pirates Organization.

In his free time, Randy enjoys trail running, reading, fishing, and traveling. He and his wife Laura live in Sharpsburg, Georgia, and they have four daughters, Hannah, Sarah, Rebekah, and Katherine. You can find Randy on social media @randygravitt or connect with him at www.randygravitt.com.

Stay In Touch

For more resources to help you
create traction in your life
and leadership visit

THEUNSTUCKBOOK.COM

Index

purpose of, 172
role of, 141
transaction formula at,
175–177
vocational, 99

T
Tensions, 194, 196–197
Traction formula
application of, 71, 188–189
components of, 50,
143–144
for contribution phase,
163–165, 169–175
for excitement phase,
152–154
for fundamentals phase,
160–162
life skills for, 145
for misery phase, 180–182
redirection in, 104–105
for renewal phase, 116–117,
185–187, 190–191
STOP signs and, 175–177

understanding of, 147
working of, 144
Truth, 179

U
UNSTUCK retreats, 142

W
Water line example, 206–208
Wisdom phase
application of, 195–199
characterization of, 115, 193
lessons of, 193–194
purpose of, 118–119
Work
by-products of, 185
heart of, 230
leaders, 206–208
misery of, 55, 187, 213–214
passion for, 169, 212–213
routine of, 52–53
understanding, 187
wisdom and, 194
work of, 208